How to Get a Job after 45

The Daily Telegraph

How to Get a Job after 45

SECOND EDITION

Julie Bayley

KOGAN PAGE

First published in 1990
Second edition 1992

Apart from any fair dealing for the purposes of research or private study, or criticism or review, as permitted under the Copyright, Designs and Patents Act, 1988, this publication may only be reproduced, stored or transmitted, in any form or by any means, with the prior permission in writing of the publishers, or in the case of reprographic reproduction in accordance with the terms of licences issued by the Copyright Licensing Agency. Enquiries concerning reproduction outside those terms should be sent to the publishers at the undermentioned address:

Kogan Page Limited
120 Pentonville Road
London N1 9JN

© Julie Bayley 1990, 1992

British Library Cataloguing in Publication Data

A CIP record for this book is available from the British Library.

ISBN 0-7494-0871-5

Typeset by DP Photosetting, Aylesbury, Bucks
Printed and bound in Great Britain by
Clays Ltd, St Ives plc.

Contents

Introduction   9

Part 1. Preparing for the Next Move

1. **Facing the Facts**   13

2. **A Realistic Approach**   18
   Age and employment *19*; Getting to know your own area *21*; Updating skills *22*; Financial implications *23*

3. **Working It Out For Yourself**   28
   Looking back *28*; Changing values *30*;
   Life management *30*; Fit for work? *31*;
   Drawing together *33*; Assessing skills *35*;
   Bridging *38*; Further information and help *38*

4. **Promoting Yourself**   39
   Analysing advertisements *40*; Letters *42*;
   Preparing a CV *46*; Application forms *52*;
   Applying 'on spec' *53*; Interviews *57*;
   Further information and help *60*

Part 2. Options

5. **Job Opportunities**   63
   Office/Administrative *64*; Practical *68*; Caring *70*;
   Teaching/Training/Guidance *74*; Sales *77*;

Security and protective services, law and order *78*;
Further information and help *82*

6. Self-Employment — 83
Having what it takes *83*; Generating ideas *84*;
Taking all the responsibility or sharing it *86*;
Testing the market *87*; Drawing up a business plan *88*; Organisations offering advice *89*; Training *91*;
Further information and help *95*

7. Part-Time Work — 97
Why part-time? *97*; The disadvantages *98*;
Different forms of part-time work *99*;
Employment rights for part-time employees *102*;
Benefits and part-time work *104*; National
Insurance *105*; Weighing it all up *106*;
Further information and help *106*

8. Voluntary Work — 107
What you can give and gain *107*; What skills can you offer? *108*; The time it takes *110*; Voluntary work and benefits *110*; A sample of voluntary organisations *111*; Be prepared *117*; Other ways of participating in the community *117*; Further information and help *120*

9. Education and Training — 122
A change in approach *122*; Why start learning more? *123*; Choosing the right course *124*; Return to learning *126*; Ways of study *127*; Finance *132*;
Further information and help *135*

10. Government Initiatives — 136
Job search seminars *137*; Job review workshops *137*;
Travel to Interview Scheme *137*; Jobclubs *137*; Job
Interview Guarantee *138*; Courses for considering the future *138*; Training and Enterprise Councils *138*;

Courses for women returners *139*; Business and
Enterprise Services *139*; Guidance *140*; Ways of using
the schemes *140*; Case studies *140*

11. A Varied Life 143

Index 147

Introduction

It can happen to anyone. Suddenly you find yourself out of work and in an age group no one seems interested in. The family may be stunned initially and react in particularly unhelpful ways. Financial commitments may weigh heavily. Friends, finding themselves at a loss for words, avoid discussing the situation. Objective help is hard to find and it is definitely too soon to retire.

Unemployment may have come as a result of redundancy, dismissal, early retirement, family commitments, ill health or choice. Whatever the cause, the solutions are never easy. The first step is to come to terms with the situation, to realise you are not alone and that your chances of getting back into work are good. With the decline in the number of school leavers entering the job market the opportunities for the older person are greatly improved.

This book aims to help you sort out the type of job you really want and to make the best possible application. There are many questions to ask yourself before making a decision and a range of opportunities to consider. It is very important to take enough time to think about what you want out of work and then to look at what you have to offer in terms of skills and experience. Older people may have been overlooked in the past but the future needs them. What might seem like a disaster at the time may well turn into a fresh start.

Part 1 Preparing for the Next Move

CHAPTER 1
Facing the Facts

In the 1930s and 40s there were very few organisations to turn to for help and advice. People tended to keep their problems to themselves or within the family. What a contrast to the openness of the 60s, when everyone began to be aware of the need for counselling and advisory services. Perhaps this is one of the reasons why older people in particular, suddenly faced with redundancy and unemployment, find it difficult to talk about their reactions.

You may feel totally isolated and as if you are the only one struggling to cope with anger, rejection, humiliation, bitterness, panic and unfulfilment. Although each situation is different, it does help to recognise that others feel the same way. Consider, for a moment, the situations these people found themselves in.

Case studies

When **George** was 51, he decided to leave his job as site manager with a building contractor because he was very unhappy in his work. He had spent ten years with a medium-sized family firm and found the personal relations side increasingly stressful. For some time before he left, he had been considering alternatives and felt his best prospects lay in self-employment. He was interested in manufacturing fencing. The final straw was when he found an important area of his work had been handed over to the boss's son who had just joined the firm after leaving college. George left.

He certainly felt relieved to be out of a nightmare working situation, though he was not at all sure about the future. He was very concerned about money. Two of his four children were working but the other two were at college and not financially independent. His wife and children knew that he had been very unhappy in his job and wanted to leave, but when he did, it nevertheless hit them like a bombshell. They did not seem to understand him. George found it very difficult to talk to his friends about it; they were in good jobs and he felt they had no idea what it was really like for him. It became an embarrassment.

Suddenly, he was at home all day on his own. His wife had a full-time job and left the house early each morning. On bad days George felt like 'curling himself in a ball'. There were various jobs that needed doing in the house but everything cost money and it was irksome to be drawing on savings all the time. No one really encouraged him to go forward with his plans for starting his own business, but when he went to the Jobcentre to look at vacancies there was nothing for his age group there.

The early weeks were bad, but George clung to his belief that his chances were not finished and pressed on with setting up his own business with the help of the Enterprise Allowance.

Madge had worked in the same firm for 25 years and when her department was closed down and she was made redundant, it felt like the end of the world. She was proud of the terraced house which she had bought and for which she was paying off a mortgage, but without work she wondered what on earth to do. Unemployment benefit was not going to stretch far. Panic set in, with sleepless nights and endless days. Madge's life had revolved round work; her friends, all her social activities, everything seemed to her to have disappeared with the job. Alone in the house, there was no one to talk to.

She went to the Jobcentre most days but there never seemed to be anything suitable and as time went by she felt her confidence slipping away. She went out less and less and became very depressed. She cut back on food shopping, desperately worried about her financial situation. She did not dare break into her redundancy payment.

Fortunately for Madge, not all her friends had disappeared. One, in particular, tried hard to help and eventually succeeded in persuading her to go along to the careers service and ask for help and advice, instead of just looking at the vacancies. This was the turning point for Madge. She felt she was being considered as a person and she gradually began to regain her self-respect.

Looking back, it was definitely the worst time of her life.

Robert left his job in the south of England for family reasons. His marriage was breaking up and he decided to get out of a very unhappy domestic situation and move back to the Midlands where his elderly widowed mother lived. He had been working as a maintenance engineer with a well-known group of hotels. Previously he had spent 15 years in the army with the parachute regiment.

Robert has been unemployed for three years and says he is becoming very sceptical. Employers, in his opinion, are looking for paper qualifications at the expense of experience and this is denying people who are able to do the job the chance to prove themselves. He feels that firms are often very irresponsible about low wages, making it impossible for people with rents, mortgages or family commitments to take jobs. Many employers do not seem to realise that some people have to count the cost of going to work as opposed to staying at home: buying suitable working clothes, travel, buying a coffee in the canteen and possibly a round of drinks for workmates in the pub.

After a time Robert said he became lethargic and found himself putting things off to another day. He became more inflexible about what he would consider doing. Sometimes he felt he was being spied on and the future looked bleak. When he was recommended to join a Jobclub he felt he was being pushed into something against his will. However, once he was there he found he was respected as a person again and the contact with others and encouragement he was given were very positive and stimulating.

'I'm the wrong age, at the wrong time, in the wrong part of the country,' said **Jock**, who would like to get into property sales. He spent most of his working life in Africa and came back to this country because of the political situation and for family reasons. He has had considerable experience of property sales but has no qualifications.

He has been trying very hard to find work and said, 'Anyone who thinks I don't want to work must be stark staring mad.' He has no friends because he cannot afford to mix with people. Buying a round of drinks in the local pub is out of the question. He goes through moods of anger and frustration and sometimes despairs of breaking down barriers. Jock talked about feeling that he 'has been completely put on the scrap heap'. He would be prepared to work for six months for half salary or even for nothing if only someone would give him the chance to prove himself.

Many women whose work has been in the home bringing up a family and then, perhaps, looking after ageing parents, experience some of these feelings when family commitments suddenly disappear and they find themselves no longer needed. If you are in this situation you will feel, in a sense, redundant. You feel fed up with being taken for granted and you want to do something in your own right. But what? You may have few, if any, qualifications and your last experience of work may have been a long time ago. Alternatively, you have the qualifications but feel so rusty and out of touch that you do not know where to begin.

It is much better to talk about your situation than to bottle up all the very natural and often strong reactions you experience. It is paving the way for the next positive step of making decisions and planning. A man in his late forties made redundant from a large engineering firm described how he suppressed his anger for 18 months, giving outsiders the impression that he was coping coolly and methodically with restructuring his life. When his anger did break through the surface, it was all the more difficult to cope with because of the time gap. It clearly affected him and his family severely.

It is often easier to talk freely to someone outside the family circle. There are several organisations that can help by giving you the chance to discuss your situation with a trained counsellor or adviser who will listen carefully to what you have to say, without making judgements or assumptions, and who will have information about opportunities that may well be of interest to you. An outsider can often be the one who starts rebuilding your confidence and self-esteem.

Your Jobcentre will be able to tell you how to contact the organisations in your area. Ask them about the following:

- Adult guidance services. Private guidance services are advertised in the Yellow Pages
- Careers service. Most careers services are now giving guidance and information to adults as well as young people. Careers service libraries are open to all
- Jobcentre client advisers. They are in a very good position to give you information about local job opportunities
- Jobclubs. Jobclubs help you apply for jobs. They also provide an

opportunity to talk to others in a similar situation and to share experiences

Unemployment brings many people face to face with a gap between ambition and attainment, one which seems to be an ever-widening gulf. Earlier ambitions may have been unrealistically high and this is the time to take stock and review the situation. It will take time and patience but will be of far greater benefit than making hasty decisions out of panic.

Unemployment changes day-to-day life and future expectations out of all recognition. Once you have accepted the fact and talked openly about how you feel, it is time to move on and look at the employment scene. That, as everyone knows, has changed too.

CHAPTER 2
A Realistic Approach

Gone are the days when it was normal practice for people to spend all their working lives with the same firm. Today's young people are being prepared for a very different working life, one which might involve moving from job to job and training and retraining as one skill is superseded by another. This change of approach hits hard at older people finding themselves out of work because it is a reversal of many or all the ideas they were brought up with. It is one thing to grow up prepared for it, but quite another to find yourself suddenly pitched into it in your late forties or fifties.

Today we are changing from an industrial society to one where the service and information industries dominate. Our manufacturing output may increase but it is likely to do so with a much smaller workforce than previously required. People are once again being replaced, this time by new technology, as we move further and further away from labour-intensive businesses. The unions have tried to resist some of these changes but with little success.

This change, together with government policy, has resulted in massive redundancies and very high unemployment. Although the national unemployment rate is now falling, the levels across the country are vastly different. We read about serious skill shortages and the need for more training; about employers in one part of the country desperate for labour, and unemployed people in another desperate for work; about the widening gap between the 'haves' and 'have-nots'. The situation is full of contradictions and the future, as always, is uncertain.

However, one change gradually taking place will be very much to the advantage of the older person: by 1995 there will be one million fewer 16-19 year olds in Britain than there were in 1988 and employers are becoming very aware of the implications of this. Britain has been a youth-orientated society for a long time, but the predicted shortage of young people in the near future is bound to force a change in attitude towards older people – an attitude which the Institute of Personnel Management claims has led to 'a vast wastage of human resources'. Economic forces will be far more instrumental in bringing about change than any legislation which might make it illegal for age to be considered in employment decisions.

Employers will need to rely more and more on the older person. Already some national retailers, supermarkets and fast-food chains are advertising for people over 50 to take on some of the routine work that has previously been done by youngsters. The scope and level of opportunities for the older person will develop in the next few years.

Age and employment

Even though the outlook is much more favourable, there are still difficulties for the older person. Some employers will take longer than others to change their attitude and we are concerned with now, not with five years hence. Employers who discriminate on the grounds of age do so for several reasons. We need to examine some of these reasons in order to work at ways of overcoming them.

Qualifications. These days exams and qualifications are thought to be of supreme importance. Any new skill which people learn has to carry with it a certificate. Sometimes these certificates mean very little in comparison with good experience but from the employment angle they mean a lot. They can mean the difference between being offered an interview or not.

People who are now in their late forties and fifties grew up in a time when qualifications were not necessarily so vital. Certainly, the apprenticeship system was thriving and this usually included passing City and Guilds examinations, but there were many skilled jobs where qualifications were less important than having the right attitude and building up experience. As a result, there are many people in this age group who have held skilled and responsible jobs for many years but have nothing on paper to prove it, apart from a reference. The reference, therefore, becomes doubly important and needs to be more detailed than is normally the case so that it shows your next employer the level of ability and responsibility you reached. If your reference does not do this, go back to your last employer if you can and explain why you need more detail. Providing you left on good terms he should understand and cooperate in this respect.

Starting a new job will probably mean *working with people younger than yourself*, taking instructions even from someone no older than your children. Employers often see this as more of a problem than it really is. It may be irksome initially, but most of us can come to terms with the situation without too much difficulty. What is important is that you convince the employer that you will be able to do so. Make a point, if you can, of telling him that you have worked well with people both younger and older than yourself.

Another fear that employers sometimes have is that an older person will be too set in his ways, unlike a younger person who can be trained in the ways of the firm. Experience is going to be your strongest selling point, but it must be tempered by a *willingness to adapt to new situations* and to learn from others. Most employers are certainly not looking for someone to come in and try to alter all their systems and procedures! Admittedly, there may be times when you have to bite your tongue and accept something you feel you could improve! People do tend to become less flexible the older they get and this can be of real concern to an employer, so it is important to be aware of this and overcome it.

You may be applying for a job that has a much *lower salary* than your last one. There are many occasions when this is necessary and you will have worked out how little you can afford to work for. Employers can be suspicious of this and start thinking of reasons for your willingness to settle for a lower salary that are

A Realistic Approach

often far from the truth! It is clearly one of the most important aspects of a job, and if you have decided to take a drop in salary, convince an employer that you have thought it through and know what you are doing.

These are some of the factors that can build up the so-called 'age barrier'. Recognising what they are is very important when trying to overcome this barrier and make age work *for* rather than against you. Recognising the jobs that are more suitable for older people is important too and we will be looking at some of these later on. But, first, what are the opportunities in your area?

Getting to know your own area

Often, we do not really know what is going on in our own backyard. Life has probably been too busy to keep up with all but the most newsworthy of local developments and, anyway, it has not seemed very important. Now it is. You may well have to start a different type of job and you need to know where the growth areas are.

Time is something you do have, so try to collect as much information as you can from as many different sources as possible. Here are a few suggestions:

- The *Employment Gazette*. This publication is available in reference libraries and gives a breakdown of employment figures on a regional basis. It comments on current employment trends and is well worth referring to. It is a Department of Employment publication and comes out monthly
- *Jobcentres*. Study the job advertisements. Talk to a client adviser about the local employment situation. You might ask these questions:
    - What have been the major changes in employment in the area?
    - What jobs are most frequently advertised now?
    - Are any companies shortly moving to the area and will they be recruiting staff through the Jobcentre?
- The *careers service*. Many careers services now offer guidance and help to adults as well as young people. Careers officers

have good local employment knowledge as well as information about education and training
- *Employment agencies*
- *Newspapers.* You will have combed the local newspapers for suitable jobs many times, but try making an analysis of the jobs advertised on one or two days by considering these points:
  - There may be hundreds of jobs advertised but how many lie within travelling distance for you?
  - Look at the number of part-time jobs advertised
  - Look at which of the following occupational areas the majority of jobs fall into: manufacturing (including engineering), construction (including electrical work, plumbing, painting and decorating etc), retail, clerical, domestic, catering, repairs/maintenance, health, education, finance, property, transport
- *Talking to people.* Pooling information with friends and acquaintances

You may consider moving to another area, in which case you will need to find out about job opportunities from scratch rather than updating your knowledge. Whichever situation you are in you will have a far clearer picture of what is available if you follow up these suggestions. Make sure that you do not make your 'travel-to-work' area too restricting. It may well be necessary to travel further to your next job: this could be one of the compromises you have to make.

Updating skills

Find out, too, about opportunities in your area to attend courses. There may be disadvantages to being in such a qualification-orientated age but there are some useful spin-offs. Colleges of further education have always provided full-time courses lasting one or two years and day release for people in employment, but they are now offering short courses to adults who need to update skills or retrain completely. The colleges are changing their approach to meet the needs of the community and are developing opportunities for the mature student. Alternatively, you may have an Adult/Community Education Centre near you which runs courses specifically for mature students.

If you have never used a computer it could be an appropriate time to join a course offering a general introduction to computing. So many jobs involve using a computer in one way or another. Word processors are taking over from typewriters in most offices and anyone looking for office work who has not been using a word processor would be well advised to get some hands-on experience. If you are considering self-employment, what about taking a course in bookkeeping or marketing?

At the moment you may not have to pay course fees at a college of further education if you are unemployed, in receipt of benefit and studying for less than 21 hours a week. Your place may, however, depend on there being a vacancy on the course and at some colleges fee-paying students take precedence. Colleges usually have a member of staff who will discuss suitable courses and fees with you and give guidance.

If there is no college within a reasonable distance of home you could consider taking an Open Learning course. Most colleges and training organisations offer Open Learning as an alternative method of study. Once you have chosen an appropriate course you take home the course books and study in your own time. You are usually assigned a tutor who arranges times to meet and discuss your progress. Alternatively, you may rely on the phone.

Look out, too, for courses advertised in the Jobcentre. Your local Training and Enterprise Council may fund courses for unemployed people wanting to retrain or those planning to start their own businesses.

We will be looking at some of the courses available in more detail in Chapter 9.

Financial implications

Your financial situation will probably play a major part in any future planning. Most people finding themselves unemployed are beset by money problems. If you have been receiving a steady salary for 30 years or so and this is suddenly cut off, you are bound to be very badly hit. You may still have considerable financial commitments and a way of life that does not adapt easily to the limitations of Unemployment Benefit.

Make sure that you are receiving all the benefits you are entitled to. The client advisers at your local Jobcentre will give you help and advice. You may be entitled to Income Support and Housing Benefit as well as Unemployment Benefit. Each situation is considered individually, so there should be no mistakes, but it is up to you to check and establish your own rights. Remember there are certain conditions that you have to abide by when receiving Unemployment Benefit:

- You must be available for work and actively seeking it
- If you do any kind of work, paid or unpaid, you must let the Unemployment Benefit Office know

Those who are receiving a vocational pension or who have had substantial redundancy payments should consult the bank manager, an accountant or an investment consultant for advice on the best way to manage their money. Firms involved in large-scale redundancies usually bring in consultants before the employees leave to give them the chance to obtain professional advice. It goes without saying that you should check carefully that any investment consultant you approach is experienced and reliable.

Most people will have to take a hard look at ways of cutting back on expenditure. Working out a practical budget should involve any members of the family who will be affected to avoid any later misunderstandings. Priorities may have to change just as expectations do. It all leads to working out carefully what you hope to make of the next 10 to 15 years. The following tables can be used as a guide when working out a budget.

A Realistic Approach

Budget planner

INCOME

£

After tax income from employment:
   PAYE earnings
   Freelance and self-employed earnings

After tax income from savings and investments

Any other income – such as Child Benefit or other State benefits, alimony or child maintenance payments, income from investment property   _____

TOTAL INCOME   _____

EXPENDITURE

Essentials   £
   Food
   Mortgage or rent
   Water rates
   Community charge/Council tax
   Electricity
   Gas
   Other fuels
   Telephone
   National Insurance contributions
   Pension contributions
   House maintenance
   Buildings and house contents insurance
   Travel to work
   Child care
   Clothes   _____

Total essential expenditure   _____

Non-essentials £
    Holidays
    Drink and cigarettes
    Entertaining and meals out
    Presents
    Car purchase
    Car maintenance
    Car insurance and road tax
    Petrol
    Travel not already allowed for
    School or college fees
    Home improvements
    Housekeeping
    Professional fees
    Trade union dues or subscriptions to professional bodies
    Life insurance
    Regular savings plans
    Personal Equity Plans
    Other investments acquired
    Newspapers, books and periodicals
    TV rental and/or licence
    Hobbies
    Loan repayments
    Bank and credit card interest
    Children's pocket money
    Your own pocket money

Total non-essential expenditure

TOTAL EXPENDITURE

EXCESS (OR OTHERWISE) OF INCOME OVER EXPENDITURE

Budget planner © Anthea Masey, *Managing Your Money*, 2nd edition, 1989 (Kogan Page).

The Department of Employment and the Central Office of Information issue leaflets and booklets which explain clearly all about benefits and how to claim them. Leaflets are available from any Jobcentre or from:

Leaflets Unit
PO Box 21
Stanmore
Midlesex HA7 1AY

Other sources of help and advice are:

- Freeline Social Security (free telephone enquiry service) 0800 666555
- Jobcentres. Unemployment Benefit Offices and Jobcentres have been combined. They give advice and information on benefit rights
- Housing Department: Information on rates and rent
- Citizens' Advice Bureau: You will be sure of a sympathetic and understanding ear and accurate information.

CHAPTER 3
Working It Out For Yourself

How many people do you know who are really happy in their work? There are plenty of people whose jobs have failed to live up to expectations and far fewer who find their work interesting and satisfying all the time.

Working out what you would like to achieve can be difficult. It means questioning much of what has been important up to this point and accepting the fact that your expectations for the next 10 to 15 years will be very different from those at the beginning of your career. The exercises in this chapter are intended to help you clarify your priorities by presenting you with some of the important issues that need to be considered carefully. After all, you do have the bonus of choice.

Let's start by looking at your last job. It can be difficult to think about it objectively, but try to imagine you are someone else evaluating the work you were doing. Ask yourself what the job was really like and what happened to you. How did others see you fitting into the role? It is important to be honest with yourself and to avoid falling into the traps of being too defensive or running yourself down. Give yourself time to think carefully about these points before moving on to the first exercise, which is the start of a bridge from your past to your future.

Looking back

The aim of this exercise is to identify:

1. aspects of work you want to keep
2. aspects you want to change

Working It Out For Yourself

Think carefully about each question. Tick the appropriate box

	YES	NO	SOMETIMES
Did you find your last job varied and stimulating?	☐	☐	☐
Was your work routine and repetitive?	☐	☐	☐
Did you find your last job stressful?	☐	☐	☐
Did you use the training you acquired when you were younger?	☐	☐	☐
Did you enjoy learning new skills?	☐	☐	☐
Were you responsible for the work of others?	☐	☐	☐
Were you satisfied with your salary?	☐	☐	☐
Did you have to work anti-social hours?	☐	☐	☐
Did you take work home with you?	☐	☐	☐
Did your work affect your family life?	☐	☐	☐
Did you work as part of a team?	☐	☐	☐
Did you get on well with your colleagues?	☐	☐	☐
Did you get on well with your boss?	☐	☐	☐
Did your job involve travelling?	☐	☐	☐
Did you have far to travel to work each day?	☐	☐	☐
Did you achieve an ambition in your last job?	☐	☐	☐
Do you feel that it is important to feel secure in order to do a job well?	☐	☐	☐

> Write down four aspects of work you feel will always be necessary and important to you and four aspects you want to change.
>
> _____
>
> _____
>
> _____
>
> _____

Changing values

Identifying particular aspects of work you enjoyed and aspects you want to change leads on to examining the way your values differ now from, let's say, 20 years ago. It is sometimes tempting to try to regain the life and work that you are used to, following the old saying, 'Better the devil you know than the devil you don't.' But even if it were possible, is it really what you want? After all, there would be something wrong if a person's needs and values stayed constant all their lives.

The aim of the exercise on pages 31–4 is to identify changes in values and priorities. While learning from the past, it is also necessary sometimes to let go of the past. It may be too late to worry about status and promotion, but that does not mean you cannot achieve job satisfaction.

Life management

Once priorities are established, planning can be more constructive. The next step is to consider the balance you would like to achieve between work and leisure. Work very often leaves little time for family, friends and interests. This might be the time to give them higher priority. If you are fit and active you will want to take advantage of some of the opportunities for leisure activities that are available today. Be fair to yourself in your planning. Consider discussing this exercise with the family and seeing what their reaction is.

What else do you want to do apart from 'work' in the next ten years? Some of the following activities or needs may be

Working It Out For Yourself

important to you. Select those that are and add any others that are not included. Decide which you want to allow more time for. Allocate marks out of 10 (0 = not important, 10 = most important).

Activities/needs	Marks out of 10
Time with the family	
Meeting/making friends outside work	
Improving the home	
Gardening	
Sport	
Reading	
Getting involved in the community	
Studying for pleasure, eg evening classes	
Open College, Open University	
Travel	
Relaxation	
Keeping up with current affairs	

Write down four activities on which you would definitely like to spend more time.

_____

_____

_____

_____

How to Get a Job After 45

Tick the appropriate box

Values	IMPORTANT	20 YEARS AGO OF SOME IMPORTANCE	NOT IMPORTANT
Job satisfaction	☐	☐	☐
Status	☐	☐	☐
Money	☐	☐	☐
Promotion	☐	☐	☐
Challenge	☐	☐	☐
Responsibility	☐	☐	☐
Pressure	☐	☐	☐
Making decisions	☐	☐	☐
Variety	☐	☐	☐
Security	☐	☐	☐
Place of work	☐	☐	☐
Being your own boss	☐	☐	☐
Being part of a team	☐	☐	☐
Friendship	☐	☐	☐
Learning	☐	☐	☐
Creativity	☐	☐	☐

Write down four values that you feel would be important to you in future work.

_____
_____
_____
_____

Fit for work?

Few of us are fit for all types of work. There are many people, for example, who have back trouble and should not be considering work which involves lifting or standing for long periods. Health is an important issue to consider when planning the future.

The aim of this exercise is to think how some of these very common health problems could affect choice of work.

Do you suffer from any of these?	How could this affect choice of work?
Skin trouble (eg dermatitis)	
Chest trouble (eg asthma)	
Heart trouble	
Poor eyesight	
Nervous disorders (eg nervous breakdown)	
Severe headaches	
Diabetes	
Epilepsy	
Arthritis	
Back trouble	
Hernia	
Hay fever	
Poor hearing	
Varicose veins	
Other considerations	

Drawing together

By now you have given careful thought to some of the aspects of work you feel will be important, to the balance you would like to achieve between work and leisure and to any constraints that health might impose. The years ahead are going to be very valuable. Work will be an important part of life but not the whole of it.

Before going further and looking at your experience and skills, bring together the factors that you have identified as being important for your future way of life.

Aspects of your last job you would like to continue
Priorities/ Values
Activities outside work
Health constraints

Working It Out For Yourself

Assessing skills

You may be considering a number of alternatives such as a particular type of work, self-employment, franchising or part-time work. Before making any decisions you must look carefully at the experience and skills you can bring to a new job.

You will probably be looking for a change of occupation, particularly if new technology has made you redundant. Your initial training and qualifications may no longer be as relevant as your work experience. You may have developed valuable skills you certainly did not have when you started work but which you now take for granted. These skills often become the main selling point for the older person and they need to be identified.

They may include:

Instructing/teaching	Driving long distances
Report writing	Using the telephone effectively
Retrieving information	Computing
Planning	Ability to work on your own
Negotiating	Dealing with the public
Representing a body of opinion	Handling difficult situations
Organisation	Counselling/advice giving
Managing the work of others	Public speaking
Setting targets	

There are plenty of others.

Think back to a typical week in your last job and make a list of all the skills you had to use in the course of your work. It is very important to make good use of this information when you come to write your CV and letters of application (see pages 42-56). This is really where you should score over a younger person. You will realise more fully what a great deal you have to offer.

Have you thought of the personal qualities your work demanded? Personal qualities may sound vague, but they too need to be identified in order to present a more complete picture to a prospective employer. They may include:

35

Outgoing personality	Determination
Energy and drive	Understanding
Punctuality	Authority
Adaptability	Conscientious approach
Patience	Initiative
Motivation	Inventiveness
Willingness	

You may have other personal qualities that are not selling points but need to be taken into consideration when deciding on your next step. For example, a person who is over-anxious is unlikely to be suitable for self-employment.

Make a list of those qualities you want to bring out in a letter of application or an interview.

It is easy to overlook the skills that are developed outside work but they can be equally important. If you belong to a club it is possible that you will have been on the committee and had a particular responsibility – for example, chairing a meeting, writing minutes, putting forward proposals, allocating work, typing, raising money. If you have been looking after an elderly relative you may have found yourself in the role of nurse, counsellor, financial adviser. DIY enthusiasts have easily identifiable skills. Some voluntary work, eg the Samaritans, provides very good training.

Make a list of your activities and interests and beside each one write down the skills you have used.

Qualifications can be very important, too. Many people pick up additional qualifications in the course of their working life. The next exercise brings together qualifications, skills and personal qualities used in work and other activities. It is useful to ask a friend or member of the family for an outside opinion of your skills and personal qualities and to fill in the third section. This will form the basis of your new or revised curriculum vitae (CV). If you already have a CV, ask yourself whether it really portrays your full potential.

Employment. List different jobs with different employers or within the same firm
Qualifications
Additional skills acquired
Personal qualities
Other activities
Another person's opinion of skills and personal qualities

Bridging

You are closer to crossing safely the bridge from the past to the future when you have thought through the issues raised in this chapter. A better knowledge of your aims and abilities will enable you to have greater confidence and clearer judgement. The work that you have done will be the basis of your new CV and will prove invaluable in the promotion of yourself.

Further information and help

The following books are valuable for more detailed self-assessment:

Build Your Own Rainbow (Lifeskills Associates)

Returning to Work: A Practical Guide for Women (Alec Reed)

Women Working it Out (COIC)

Working it Out (Careers & Occupational Information Centre) An aid to deciding about jobs.

CHAPTER 4
Promoting Yourself

Promoting yourself means convincing an employer that you are the most suitable person for the job. Your age and previous experience must be made to work for you and in this chapter we are going to look at ways in which this can be done.

Taking first things first, as an older person you have qualities and skills to offer that a younger person has not had the time to acquire. Look at the following general points and see how many of them apply to you:

- Long experience of working with others and fitting in
- Supervisory/managerial experience
- Proven ability to work on your own
- Ability to communicate well with people at all levels
- Reliability: much less likely than a younger person to want to move away from area; children grown up, so no need to take time off for them; less pressure at home as children become independent
- Appreciation of value of work both financially and for self-fulfilment
- Motivated by wish to do a job well rather than by seeking promotion
- Good work record – awareness of importance of punctuality, confidentiality, tact
- Better able to take criticism than a younger person
- Determination developed through experience to overcome difficulties.

Apart from these general points you have the skills that were required for a particular job, identified in the last chapter. Build up a picture of yourself in the best possible light and believe in it!

Analysing advertisements

Jobs are advertised in all sorts of places, from national and local papers, trade journals, Jobcentres and employment agencies to shop windows, and noticeboards. Advertisements vary considerably in format and you might be asked to apply in one of several ways, such as:

- contacting an address or phone number
- sending a letter of application
- applying in writing enclosing a CV
- filling in an application form

Let us look at a couple of advertisements.

Example 1

West Mercia Constabulary

A vacancy will shortly exist for an
ADMINISTRATION CLERK
At the Police Station, Main Road,
Newtown
37 hour week
Salary Scale 1 commences at 21 years
Two part-time workers would be considered.
Salary scale pro rata.

Application forms, which are returnable by March 11, 1993, may be obtained by writing to: The Chief Superintendent
West Mercia Constabulary
Police Station, Main Road,
Newtown NT3 4HW
Only successful applicants will be notified in writing.

Promoting Yourself

If you read the first advertisement carefully you might come to some of these conclusions:

- No age limit is mentioned
- 'Salary Scale 1 commences at 21 years' might suggest that young applicants are likely to apply
- This is an opportunity for job sharing
- If you get the job you would probably be working with much younger people
- Once in the job there might well be opportunities for advancement
- Any previous experience of administration in a paid or unpaid capacity would be very useful in showing your administrative ability
- Working in a police station would require responsibility and confidentiality
- The job might involve using a computer. If you have not used a computer before, look out for a basic course!

Example 2

> **Ring and Ride Assistant Controller**
>
> West Midlands Special Needs Transport is committed to providing accessible door-to-door transport for the disabled.
>
> An **Assistant Controller** is required to help set up a new Ring and Ride service in Newtown with responsibility for day-to-day management including staff supervision, vehicles and passenger liaison.
>
> Management experience in transport or a related field is required together with an appreciation of the needs of those with mobility problems.
>
> Contact: John Cox
> 206-212 Main Street
> Newtown NT3 5DP
> (0800 000 0000) for details

Once again, study this advertisement carefully and see if you come to some of these conclusions:

- The job is for an *assistant* controller
- You would probably be working closely with a controller
- Together you would be setting up a new service
- You would be responsible for day-to-day management
- Some previous management experience would be necessary
- You would need to be good with people – both the staff and the disabled people for whom you are running the service
- Some of the staff might be volunteers
- If you do not have any experience of disabled people you would have to find out quickly about their problems
- The person appointed will be someone who gives staff and clients confidence and who has a friendly manner combined with good organisational ability

This careful analysis of an advertisement is essential for making a good application, because it helps you to work out what the employer is looking for. You can then match that up with your own experience and attitudes and write a well thought-out letter of application.

Letters

Most applications involve a letter: either a short letter to accompany a CV or an application form, or a longer informative letter which takes the place of forms and CVs. Some advertisements specify that letters should be handwritten. This is usually when handwriting is needed in the job, but some employers feel that the way a person's handwriting is formed can reveal useful information about that person's character and attitudes. If you have the choice, send a typed letter!

The advertisement we looked at for an administration clerk says that application forms are available from the given address and should be returned completed by a certain date. Although not essential, it is advisable to send a short letter with the completed application form. This is a way of showing the employer that you understand what he is looking for, that you

Promoting Yourself

can write a good letter and that you have taken the trouble to write it.

Here is an example of this type of letter. Preferably, it should be written on one side of unlined paper (two sides at the most).

---

10 Highfield Avenue,
Seaford SD3 4PR

The Chief Superintendent,
West Mercia Constabulary,
Police Station,
Main Road,
Newtown NT3 4HW

6 March 1993

Dear Sir,

I am very interested in working for the Police Force as a civilian and am applying for the post of **administrative clerk**.

In my previous job I worked as a member of a team and fitted in well with colleagues of different ages. I appreciate that everyone working in a police station must be completely trustworthy and responsible and can guarantee that I would be suitable in both respects.

I am enclosing my application form and look forward to hearing from you.

Yours faithfully,

(signature)
(name)

State purpose of letter
Stress interest

Select a few of the points you think the interviewer will be looking for

The advertisement for an Assistant Controller does not specify whether you need to complete an application form or send a CV but gives you a contact for further details. Let us assume that you ring Mr Cox and he asks you to write a letter outlining your previous experience and giving your reasons for wanting the job. This letter will be considerably longer than the previous one and might follow these lines:

State purpose of letter
Show enthusiasm

Add any relevant experience of helping disabled

Bring out management experience

---

10 Highfield Avenue,
Sandwell SD2 4PR

Mr J Cox,
206-212 Main Street,
Newtown NT3 5DP

5 March 1993

Dear Mr Cox,

I would like to apply for the post of Assistant Controller for West Midlands Special Needs Transport. The job sounds challenging and very worthwhile and I feel that I have the enthusiasm and commitment to carry it out.

I am particularly interested in helping disabled people and see the Ring and Ride service as a way of increasing their independence and preventing them from feeling continually indebted to family and friends.

For the last ten years I have been manager of a branch of the chain of electrical shops, Glow Bright. My work included stock control, ordering, buying, interviewing and appointing staff and serving customers. I ran the branch successfully and feel that the management experience I have had would enable me to help set up the Ring and Ride service and manage it.

Earlier in my career I was employed as a salesman in the Midlands. This brought me into contact with a wide range of people. I have a clean driving licence, good mechanical knowledge and would be quite capable of being in charge of vehicles.

I enjoy being an active member of the community and am currently helping to raise money for a much needed extension to our community centre. This has taken up most of my spare time recently.

I am very interested in this post and hope that I may be selected for interview. As a resident of the borough of Newtown I have a very good knowledge of the area. I would be prepared to put in as much extra time as required to set up the scheme successfully. I look forward to hearing from you.

Yours sincerely,

(signature)
(name)

Clean driving licence important

Mention interests or activities that are relevant, eg interest in needs of people

Local knowledge might be useful

Show that you are prepared to put in extra time to get the scheme started

The present trend is to write a CV and send it with an accompanying letter for every job application. However, if you are not specifically asked for a CV an informative letter such as the one above is more personal and gives you the chance to emphasise the points you want to make. A CV, like an application form, is restricting because of its format. It is perhaps more suitable for a person with a number of relevant paper qualifications and previous employment which relates closely to the job in question.

Preparing a CV (curriculum vitae)

A CV normally gives a person's name, address, age, marital status, educational and vocational qualifications, previous jobs, interests and the names and addresses of people prepared to give references. The purpose of a CV is to enable an employer to form a quick impression of the candidate from the facts and it is often the basis for selecting a shortlist for interview. It must, therefore, be carefully prepared and well presented. It should be typed to the highest standard and photocopied on good quality white paper or, alternatively, printed on a word processor. It should not occupy more than two sides of A4 paper as if it is too long it defeats its purpose. *Example 1* on page 47 is a fairly standard format.

There are several disadvantages to this format for an older person. It draws immediate attention to age and then goes right back to school and exams, before listing previous jobs. Working on the principle that it is a person's suitability for the job rather than age which should be the main criteria for choice, I would suggest using an alternative format. Put what matters most first and avoid aspects of your life which are no longer relevant. Irrelevant information can cloud the picture you want to present.

Example 1   **Promoting Yourself**

CURRICULUM VITAE

Name:

Address:

Telephone number:

Date of birth:

Marital status:

Nationality:

Education: Name of schools, colleges
                    Exams taken with results

Further training: Apprenticeship
                    Day-release courses
                    Other relevant training courses and certificates

Additional skills: Driving licence
                    Skills that might be relevant for the job

Previous employment: Names of employers and dates of each job. Position held in each job and brief description of responsibilities

Activities and interests: Any interests or activities outside normal work which might give a fuller picture of the person. Anything relevant to the job or that shows specialist knowledge, responsibility, caring attitude particularly important

References: Names and addresses of two people prepared to write references; at least one should be able to refer to your previous employment; the other can be more of a character reference

Example 2

<table>
<tr><td colspan="2" align="center">**CURRICULUM VITAE**</td></tr>
<tr><td>Name:</td><td></td></tr>
<tr><td>Address:</td><td></td></tr>
<tr><td>Telephone number:</td><td></td></tr>
<tr><td>Last employment:</td><td>Name of company or employer, dates of employment, position held, brief description of work and responsibilities</td></tr>
<tr><td>Previous relevant employment:</td><td>List other jobs which are relevant but do not necessarily include dates. Give most attention to the jobs that seem most relevant. (There is no need to give dates for all the jobs you list. If you do, it makes it more difficult to leave out the irrelevant or unsatisfactory ones because there will be obvious gaps – see Example 3)</td></tr>
<tr><td>Education and qualifications:</td><td>Exams taken at school or 'good general education'
College/university courses
Apprenticeship
Courses attended and certificates</td></tr>
<tr><td>Additional skills:</td><td>Skills acquired through work or activities outside work (see Chapter 3, Assessing skills)
Driving licence</td></tr>
<tr><td>Activities and interests:</td><td>As in Example 1</td></tr>
<tr><td>Age:
Nationality:
Marital status:</td><td>These can be left out but are best included</td></tr>
<tr><td>References:</td><td>As in Example 1</td></tr>
</table>

Example 3 The completed curriculum vitae

CURRICULUM VITAE

Name:	John Davies
Address:	6 High Street Mayfield MD6 1RN
Telephone:	0692 3475
Last employment: 1971–1991	STONES ENGINEERING Ltd Electronics Engineer. Section leader of Measurement Department, repairing electro-mechanical and electronic equipment together with all instrument calibrations. Responsible for planning work schedule, meeting deadlines, maintaining high standards
Previous relevant employment:	SPEED ELECTRICS Electrical/electronics maintenance in Instrument Department. Maintaining, overhauling, repairing high-speed machine tools NATIONAL SERVICE: REME Attained rank of Corporal. Served in England and Cyprus
Education and qualifications:	Good general education City and Guilds Electrical Engineering Apprenticeship with Speed Electrics Specialist training courses on control equipment for machine tools
Additional skills:	Ability to plan and organise work load and to oversee work of others Leadership – developed through work as Cub/Scout Leader Experience of committee work and taking the chair at meetings Full driving licence

Activities and interests:	Cub/Scout Leader. Interested in young people, encouraging enterprise and interest in outdoor activities Mayfield town football supporter Gardening – Chairman of local allotment association DIY.
Personal details:	Date of birth: 6.10.38 Nationality: British Marital status: Married. Three children grown up and independent
References:	Mr D Roberts Mr J Hayward Stones Engineering Ltd 10 Hillingsway Riverside Mayfield Mayfield MD6 5RN MD6 3RN

John has not included in his CV details of the time he was self-employed and started a DIY shop. He ran into financial difficulties and had to sell up after two years. He suffered a minor breakdown as a result of the pressures of the business and was unemployed for 12 months. This is not relevant to the jobs for which he is currently applying and so is best left out.

He chose his referees carefully. Mr Roberts is the Personnel Manager at Stones Engineering Ltd and is therefore able to base his reference on John's work with the firm. Mr Hayward has known John for ten years and is very well suited to write a good character reference, bringing in information about his work as a Cub/Scout leader and other activities.

In the following example, Anne makes it clear why she has not been employed for the last five years.

Example 4

	CURRICULUM VITAE
Name:	Anne Davies
Address:	6 Holly Drive Crayford Northumberland NT4 9JY
Telephone no:	0619 381942
Last employment: 1979–1987	Brown Morgan, Solicitors. Secretary to partner. Duties included drafting and typing letters, maintaining efficient filing and records systems, answering the phone, making appointments. Left post to nurse sick parents
Previous relevant experience:	Part-time secretary at local Junior School. Duties included typing letters, dealing with registers, filling in forms for education authority, collecting dinner money Clerical work with mail order firm
Education and qualifications: 1960–1962 1990	Good general education College Diploma in Secretarial Studies Typing RSA Stage 3 Word Processing RSA Stage 2 Bookkeeping RSA Stage 1
Additional skills:	First Aid Certificate Good organiser Able to get on well with people Clean driving licence
Activities and interests: 1966–1976	Bringing up family of three children

1987–1991	Looking after elderly sick parents Member of badminton club. Served on the committee Active member of Parent Teachers' Association while children were at school Attended college evening classes to update skills
Personal details:	Date of birth: 26.3.1944 Nationality: British Marital status: Divorced
References:	Mr L Brown — Dr A Hutchings Brown Morgan, — Highbridge Medical Solicitors — Centre 10 High Street — Crayford Crayford — CF3 6PR CF9 1AB

It takes time to prepare a good CV. Look back at the self-assessment exercises you did in Chapter 3 and use them to help you make the most of skills you have acquired, previous experience and personal qualities. You may have to write out your CV several times before you feel satisfied with it. It helps if you discuss it with a friend or member of the family and get another opinion.

Application forms

Application forms can be daunting if you have not had to fill one in for a very long time. There are a few golden rules to follow:

1. Read the instructions at the top of the form very carefully. You may be asked to use black ink, ball-point pen, block capitals for name and address etc. When they receive hundreds of applications, employers are known to discard those that do not conform to these instructions.
2. Read the form through once to get the general impression and

Promoting Yourself

then a second time more slowly, looking very carefully at each question.
3. Photocopy the application form and fill in the photocopy as a practice run. You may need more than one photocopy.
4. Ask someone to check through your practice run for spelling mistakes and other basic errors.
5. Make sure you send the final form off in time to ensure it arrives before the closing date.
6. Keep your rough copy so that you can look at it again before your interview. You are more than likely to be asked about points you made on your application form.

You will probably find one question on the form that asks for your reasons for wanting the job or for feeling that you are suited to it. What you write here clearly carries a lot of weight and strategy is needed! You must find out as much as you can about the job in order to answer this well: then you can be sure your reasons fit the bill. If possible, develop a link between your previous experience and the new job and above all try to convey a convincing enthusiasm. Be prepared to spend some time on this answer: write it out in rough, revise it and work out how much you can write in the given space without making it appear half empty or over crowded.

Applying 'on spec'

Many jobs are never actually advertised and if you approach an employer with a general speculative enquiry you might just be lucky. He may have been on the point of advertising a post or he may feel that you have something to offer which he is badly in need of. If you do find you have made contact with an employer at just the right time, the great advantage is that you are probably not going to find yourself up against hundreds of other applicants.

If you decide to write to an employer, your letter must make an impact. It can be quite short and accompanied by a CV, or longer if it is to be sent on its own. Let us consider a couple of speculative letters.

How to Get a Job After 45

Try to find out the manager's name

State clearly why you are writing

Develop a link between your previous experience and this job

> Springfield,
> Downing Road,
> Sunbourne
> SE6 1PR
>
> Mr P J Williams,
> AP Security Ltd,
> Liverpool Street,
> Walsall
> WS3 9BS
>
> 10 January 1993
>
> Dear Mr Williams,
>
> I am writing to enquire if you have any vacancies for security officers.
>
> For the last five years I have been in charge of a department in a large store where security has been of the utmost importance. I appreciate that you would only consider people who were honest and reliable and that you would need to check out references. My CV is enclosed, including the names and addresses of two referees.
>
> I would be happy to work irregular hours and would be prepared to work part time or full time. I have a clean driving licence and am physically fit.
>
> I would very much like to have the opportunity to talk to you about employment prospects in security work and look forward to hearing from you.
>
> Yours sincerely,
>
> (signature)
> (name)

Show an understanding of what the employer is likely to want

Flexible approach

Try to encourage a response!

Promoting Yourself

Here is a longer letter without a CV to a training organisation.

Find out the manager's name — *Show that you have some knowledge of the work* — *Your unemployment will be an advantage in this case*

> Winterbourne,
> Forest Road,
> Sunbury
> SE6 1PR
>
> Mrs R G Edwards,
> Newby Training Organisation,
> Bakewell Street,
> Gloucester
>
> 10 January 1993
>
> Dear Mrs Edwards,
>
> I am very interested in the work being done by the Newby Training Organisation and am writing to enquire if you have any vacancies.
>
> Since being made redundant I have been attending a Jobclub and have talked to many unemployed people about their need to update their skills and raise their level of confidence. Being unemployed has given me a greater understanding of the problems and I feel that I could make a valuable contribution to courses designed to help unemployed people get back to work.
>
> My previous job was under-manager in a 40-bedroomed hotel which has recently been taken over. We employed 15 staff, full time and part time, and had two YT trainees. It was my responsibility to monitor the trainees' work experience and training. I was also jointly responsible with the manager for interviewing and appointing staff. This has given me an awareness of the needs of the employer and the importance of training.

> I would very much like to discuss employment possibilities with you and look forward to hearing from you.
>
> Yours sincerely,
>
>
> (signature)
> (name)

Looking forward to a reply and meeting!

Alternatively, you can telephone an employer and try to arrange an appointment with him or her, an approach that is more likely to succeed with a small firm rather than a large one. It helps if you can say you have been advised to contact him by a third person (but obviously this is not often possible). Avoid asking directly on the phone if there are any vacancies. Instead, try this line:

You:	Good morning, Mr Davies. My name is Jane Bennett and I'm ringing you to ask if I could come and see you to ask your advice about job opportunities in horticulture.
Employer:	Well, I've no vacancies and I'm pretty busy at the moment.
You:	I thought I would contact you because you probably have the best overall picture of the horticultural trade in this area.
Employer:	Mm ...
You:	I realise you are very busy and I wouldn't want to take up more than ten minutes of your time.
Employer:	I don't think I can be of any help.
You:	Well, could I possibly come along at a time to suit you to ask you one or two questions?
Employer:	All right.

It can be an uphill task and it takes considerable skill to keep the conversation going! If you succeed in making an appointment,

Promoting Yourself

plan your approach very carefully so that you get as much information and help as possible in a short time. Never stay too long. With any luck, the employer will be impressed by you and bear you in mind when he next has a suitable vacancy. A mature, quietly confident approach will make its mark.

Interviews

How long ago did you last have an interview? A long time? Well, once you have been offered an interview you could be half way to the job, so it is worth spending time preparing and practising. Yes, practising! If you prepare for your interview carefully, you will find it much easier to be calm at the time.

It almost goes without saying that you must find out as much as you can about the job and the company or organisation. You will have gathered some information before applying, but at this stage you should do some further research. How you will do this depends on the type of job, but here are a few suggestions:

- Large companies usually produce leaflets or brochures outlining their activities. Write to or telephone the company asking them to send you their literature.
- Look up the company in the Job Book published by CRAC each year, available in most public libraries and careers offices. If the company is large enough to be included you will find valuable information with details of the number of employees, principal activities, locations, welfare and social activities etc.
- Look up the company in your local industrial or business directory which should be available at your public library.
- If the company or organisation is open to the public, eg shop, garage, hotel, hospital etc, make sure you visit it. If the opportunity arises, talk to a member of the staff, explain that you have an interview and that you are trying to find out more about the job.
- If it is a small business, ring up the employer and ask a few carefully thought out questions to give you a fuller picture.
- Some employers are happy for people to go along for a preliminary chat before the interview.

You will feel very much more confident if you have done this. Not only will it create a good impression with the interviewer, but it will also help you when it is your turn to ask some questions.

The next step is to think about what you might be asked in the interview and work out your answers in advance. Make a list, which will probably include some of the following:

- Why did you leave your last job?
- What have you been doing while unemployed?
- Why do you think you are suitable for this job?
- In what way is your previous experience relevant?
- How would you cope with working with younger people?
- What salary were you on previously?
- How would you manage on a smaller income?
- Do you have any health problems that might affect your work?
- When could you start work?

These are general points that could apply to any job. Add to the list any questions which are relevant to the particular job you are hoping to get.

When the interviewer has covered the points he wants to make, you will probably be asked if you have any questions. You may find that questions emerge naturally from the interview, but it is as well to be prepared and have a few up your sleeve.

Think very carefully about the salary before the interview. You may already know what you would be offered if you got the job, but very often this is not the case. Consider what your response would be if you were offered less than you expected. It might be better to take the job and hope to negotiate a rise after six months; or, if that fails, you could start applying for other jobs from a position of strength. Many an interview has turned sour over the matter of salary.

Thinking about what you might say is very different from actually saying it and this is where a practice interview can be of great help. Ask a member of the family or a friend to give you a mock interview based on the questions you have worked out and adding a few surprise ones. Answers should never appear

Promoting Yourself

rehearsed or learnt by heart, but one or two practice runs can help some people to speak in a more relaxed and fluent way when under pressure.

Deciding what to wear for an interview should not be left to the day. Plan ahead so that you do not have last-minute washing and ironing or a dash to the cleaner's. The important thing is to be tidy and sensibly dressed. Remember that first appearances do count and interviewers like to see that a candidate has taken trouble.

Once the day comes, make sure you arrive at least ten minutes early. You will not get any sympathy if you are late because you lost the way! So you must plan carefully how you are going to get there. If you intend to take a bus or a train, take an earlier one than necessary so that you are covered if there is a break-down or a hold-up. If driving, allow time for traffic jams and finding a parking space. You may well find you have an hour or so to spare – but far better to fill in an hour than to arrive five minutes late.

When you are called in, the act begins! Most interviewers try to put candidates at their ease. You may even be offered a cup of coffee or a cigarette. While it is polite to accept a cup of coffee, it is a mistake to smoke in an interview. However desperate you are, you must resist the temptation.

Whatever the job, you must appear very keen to get it. Remember that you have a lot of experience behind you and a great deal to offer. Do not be put off by finding your interviewer is much younger than you. That's life!

You may feel like forgetting the interview once it is over, but unless you have been offered the job on the spot it is a good idea to consider how it went. Interviews definitely improve with practice, particularly if you analyse points which you felt did not come out in your favour and try to improve on them next time. Ask yourself if there was a turning point in the interview and if so, what caused it. Think back to questions that seemed difficult at the time and consider how you could have answered them. Remember, an interview is never a waste of time. At best, it leads to the offer of a job; if this is not the case, it is very good practice for the one that will land the job.

Further information and help

Jobhunt MSC leaflets: 1. *Get That Job* 2. *Be Your Own Boss* 3. *Getting Back to Work*

CVs and Written Applications, Judy Skeats (Ward Lock)

How to Interview and be Interviewed, Michele Brown and Gyles Brandreth (Sheldon Press)

Great Answers to Tough Interview Questions: How to Get the Job You Want, 3rd edition, Martin John Yate (Kogan Page)

The Interview Game – and How It's Played, Celia Roberts (BBC Publications)

Part 2 Options

CHAPTER 5
Job Opportunities

There are many occupations which are clearly suited to young people for a variety of reasons. Cabin crews on airlines, professional athletes and beauticians are usually in their twenties or thirties.

There are other jobs, though, which an older person might feel are suitable but which are often given to young people in order to create a youthful image. Take, for example, a local government tourism officer, responsible for promoting tourism in the area. This job requires among other things a good knowledge of the district, imaginative ideas, the ability to communicate well with people and good organisational skills: qualities which are not age related, yet posts like this often go to people well under forty. Similarly, estate agents usually employ young people as salesmen despite the fact that maturity and experience in life would seem to have great relevance. It is good to be aware of these trends, because they might influence the way you write a letter of application or what points you try to bring out in an interview.

There is more logic behind employment trends in the computing field. It is very difficult to enter computer programming over the age of 30 because of the nature of the work and the fact that the industry is changing fast. Computer operators require good eyesight and manual dexterity as well as the ability to work under pressure, and are usually in their twenties or thirties.

It is not only the nature of the work that makes certain jobs age related, it is the training involved too. Employers will weigh up the cost of a lengthy training against the return that can be expected and this can be limiting for older people. Lengthy retraining, therefore, is rarely realistic.

Some occupations offer only a very low income to new entrants, regardless of previous experience. This can be another barrier for the older person.

There are, however, no hard and fast rules. Present employment trends do not bar a person from applying for anything, but it is likely to be more rewarding to apply for those jobs that offer the best chances to someone with maturity and experience. Remember, too, that trends can change; what is fashionable one year may well be different the following year.

The jobs listed in this chapter are all possibilities for someone looking for a change of occupation. Some, such as teaching and social work, involve initial training, but most are jobs where experience and skills gained in previous employment can be transferred to a new situation. Skilled craft jobs such as plumbing, carpentry etc are not included because they are not a very realistic option for someone in their late forties or fifties to take up. However, in some jobs, such as caretaking, DIY skills developed as a hobby are important. The list is not comprehensive – no list can be – but it aims to provide a few new ideas to those not sure of which direction to take.

Certain jobs can be grouped together because they require similar skills and interests. The jobs in this chapter are grouped under six general headings: office/administrative; practical; caring; teaching/training/guidance; sales; security and protective services/law and order.

Office/Administrative

To be suitable for a job in this category you will probably:

- be a good organiser
- be confident when talking to people you do not know
- have a good telephone manner
- be neat, accurate and methodical in your approach to work
- enjoy a job that is mainly office based

Job Opportunities

Automobile Association/Royal Automobile Club
Both organisations welcome older applicants without asking for specific qualifications: they are looking for general ability and the right attitude. There are opportunities in a range of jobs including clerical, administrative work, accounts, insurance, route planning (both home and overseas), hotel inspectors (for AA and RAC hotel star ratings). Further information can be obtained from regional offices.

Civil Service
This is still one of Britain's largest employers although government cuts in the Civil Service mean fewer opportunities. Non-specialists (ie people without professional qualifications) are usually employed as administrators at different levels:

1. *Executive Officer.* There are no formal age limits but candidates of 55 or over are less likely to be appointed unless they possess exceptional experience or qualifications. Applicants must be prepared to accept responsibility and if employed in a local office will probably be dealing with the public. They must have:
   (a) 5 GCE passes, including 2 at A level. One of these passes must be in English language.
   (b) or a degree.
   Alternative equivalent qualifications will be considered individually. For further information about requirements and methods of application write to:

   Civil Service Commission   or   Civil Service Commission
   Alencon Link   Room 520
   Basingstoke   St Andrew's House
   Hampshire   Edinburgh
   RG21 1JB   EH1 3BX
   0256 29222

2. *Administrative Officer.* There is no upper age limit. The work involves support tasks, eg dealing with correspondence, staffing reception points, advising members of the public. Applicants must have 5 GCE O-level passes or School

Certificate (typing not required). Alternatively, you can take a written entrance test.
3. *Administrative Assistant.* There is no upper age limit, but most Administrative Assistants are under 30. Duties are general clerical work, which does not usually include typing. Applicants must have 2 GCE O-level passes including English language or School Certificate. Alternatively, you can take a written entrance test.

For further information about methods of application for Administrative Officers or Administrative Assistants contact your local Jobcentre.

Community Alarm assistant

Community Alarm is a system which enables old people to contact a control station by pressing a button whenever they need help. Assistants generally work shifts at a central control station, usually set up by the local Housing Department. They are responsible for answering alarm calls, talking to clients to reassure them and find out about any problems, and contacting the appropriate people for help. A friendly telephone manner and a clear voice are required. Further information can be obtained from the Housing Department.

Housing officer

Those working for local government study for the Institute of Housing's professional qualification and many entrants have a degree. However, with the growth of private housing associations, opportunities are developing for people without qualifications but with good organisational skills, the ability to deal with people and an interest in social problems. The work involves administration, maintenance and allocation of rented property. Contact local private housing associations for further details.

Local government

Non-specialists (ie people without professional qualifications) are employed as administrators at different levels and as clerical workers.

Job Opportunities

1. *Local Government Administrator.* The work involves supervising junior staff, liaising with local government officers or elected representatives of the local council and local community, report writing etc. There is no upper age limit but applicants must have the relevant qualifications or requirements. An increasing number of entrants are graduates but entry is possible with O and A levels. For further information, contact the personnel officer of any county council, district council or London borough council.
2. *Local Government Clerical Worker.* The work consists of routine clerical tasks, eg sorting correspondence, filing and updating records, compiling statistics etc (you do not need to be able to type). In some departments you will be in contact with members of the public. There is no upper age limit but many clerical workers are recruited straight from school. Educational qualifications are not essential, but the minimum preferred qualifications are 3 O levels including English.

Medical receptionist

Opportunities occur in medical general practices, dental practices and at opticians. The job involves answering the phone, making appointments, dealing with people on arrival and some clerical work. Many employers prefer mature, understanding people.

Medical records clerk

Clerks are based in hospitals and are responsible for compiling, maintaining and storing patients' medical records and making them available to medical staff. Educational qualifications are not essential; there may be an opportunity to take the AMRO (Association of Health Care Information and Medical Records Officers) certificate or diploma.

National Trust administrator

Administrators are responsible for the upkeep and daily running of National Trust property. This includes the appointment and supervision of volunteer guides etc as well as the organisation of functions, eg concerts or plays. No specific qualifications are required but good public relations skills are essential. Posts are usually residential.

For further information, contact the National Trust Head Office.

Secretary

Although the average age of secretaries is young, many employers prefer an older person. Nowadays, secretaries will probably need to use a word processor and other modern office equipment (training courses are available at colleges of further education). Personal Assistants usually have greater responsibility and may be in charge of clerical staff. Their work often involves making travel arrangements, organising meetings, conferences and social functions etc.

Practical

You may well identify with some of the following points if you are suited to practical work:

- you enjoy working with your hands
- you prefer getting on with the job in hand to sorting out paperwork
- your hobbies include DIY, gardening, driving etc
- you dislike being in one room all day
- you are calm and methodical

Florist

Artistic flair is needed but there are no academic requirements. Many colleges of further education run day-release courses in floristry. You need to have nimble fingers, stamina and the ability to work to deadlines. There are opportunities for part-time work at busy times such as weekends, when wedding orders are being made up.

Glass-house grower

There are often opportunities for seasonal work, such as pricking out seedlings, potting etc, at a nursery or garden centre. Nimble fingers and patience are required.

Job Opportunities

Hospital driver
Hospitals generally run a small transport fleet for collecting goods and materials, delivering blood samples, collecting rubbish etc. This work is particularly suitable for people with previous driving employment experience. (NB. This is *not* the Ambulance Service which rarely considers applicants over 35.)

Hospital porter
The work involves taking patients to different parts of the hospital, delivering stores, collecting and delivering equipment, the distribution of meals to wards etc. Applicants must be physically fit, good with people and prepared to work shifts.

Housekeeper
Housekeepers are responsible for the domestic services in hotels, hospitals, residential homes, student accommodation and boarding schools. The work is often supervisory (overseeing cleaners, laundry, sewing etc) but housework may also be involved. Applicants must have good organisational skills, get on well with people and be physically fit.

Postwomen/Postmen
Entry is up to the age of 59. A current driving licence is required, and applicants should be reliable, prepared to start work very early and physically fit. There are no specific educational requirements, but applicants may have to take a short written test.

School caretaker
Caretakers must be able to undertake general maintenance jobs and are also responsible for moving desks, chairs etc for meetings, exams, plays, and so on. The job may involve evening and weekend work. Applicants must be physically fit and prepared to take on responsibility.

Steward of sports club, eg golf club, sailing club
Responsibilities include the upkeep of the clubhouse and supply of refreshments, including running the bar if licensed. This is

often a residential job suitable for a husband-and-wife team. Applicants should enjoy meeting people and be prepared for evening and weekend work.

Taxi driver
Driving a taxi involves working long, irregular hours. Some mechanical ability is required, and drivers must pass a medical examination (including sight and hearing tests), have a full, clean Group A UK driving licence and obtain a special licence from the local authority or, in London, Public Carriage Office. In London it is essential to know your way round in great detail, as well as to know all buildings of note; this is referred to as 'the knowledge'. A special licence is not required for private hire vehicles which are not allowed to stand or ply for hire: drivers wait at the depot between journeys. They may make longer trips, eg to airports, and be hired for weddings, funerals etc.

Undertaker's assistant
The job gives opportunities for driving, bearing at funerals and assisting with office work. Personal characteristics are very important: you must be able to cope with people in distressing situations. This is a job suitable for older applicants and often involves part-time work.

Caring

People interested in caring jobs will be:

- interested in people
- sympathetic and understanding
- able to help without becoming too emotionally involved
- confident and calm
- flexible

Blood sample collector/phlebotomist
Based in hospitals, phlebotomists are responsible for taking blood samples from the arms and fingers of adult patients and the heels of babies when requested by a medical practitioner. The work is particularly suitable for someone with laboratory or nursing

experience, but this is not essential. Requirements are physical stamina, a reassuring manner and the ability to work accurately. It is mainly part-time work. For further information contact your local health authority.

Care assistant
Care assistants give general help in residential homes, particularly those for the elderly. The job may involve lifting and working unsocial hours. There is a need to be flexible in your approach to the hours and the jobs required. It is usually part-time work.

Home care assistant/nurse
Opportunities for care assistants and nurses to look after people in their own homes can be found through private nursing organisations. The work is usually part time.

Home help/home carer/community carer
In many areas home helps have been given another name such as home carer or community carer. This reflects the change in occupation. Whereas a home help undertook cleaning and general domestic work, a home carer's role is to provide personal care to help the elderly or disabled to maintain independence in their own home. The job might include helping a person wash and dress, changing a catheter bag, settling a person down for the night etc. Domestic work might be included where necessary.

Minister of religion
There are special schemes for people of different ages and with different backgrounds in some denominations, eg the Church of England. Training varies according to the church but older applicants with a genuine commitment are welcomed.

Nursing auxiliaries/health care assistant
The work involves providing basic care under the supervision of qualified nurses: they help patients dress and undress, issue bedpans (emptying and cleaning), make beds, help feed, deal with laundry etc. There are opportunities with the National Health

Service, private hospitals, clinics and old people's homes. No qualifications are required and there is no upper age limit. People who have cared for children or parents at home can often transfer skills successfully to a wider situation in hospital.

Under 'Project 2000', nursing auxiliaries will become health care assistants and will be given more training and more responsibility.

Occupational therapy helper
Helpers assist occupational therapists. The work varies according to the type of patients (eg the elderly, young people with injuries resulting from road accidents, stroke patients, the mentally ill etc). They must be physically fit and strong as the work may involve lifting and moving patients. They should get on well with people and be able to take direction from younger members of staff. There are no specific entry requirements but health and personality are key factors.

Physiotherapy helper
He or she carries out routine patient-care tasks within precise guidelines and must be physically fit, good with people and prepared to take direction from younger members of staff.

Probation officer
A probation officer works closely with people who have been to court for committing an offence and who have been given a probation order. They have to maintain regular contact with the offender and work out a suitable programme which will help him or her cope and lead a better life. Probation officers also prepare reports to help the courts gain a fuller understanding of the defendant's background before sentencing. There is a two-year training course for graduates or non-graduates leading to the diploma in Social Work. Formal entry qualifications are not essential but evidence of ability to cope with the level of the course is required and some relevant experience.

Probation ancillaries
Probation ancillaries assist probation officers in their work. This

includes supervising people who have been sentenced by the court to carry out a certain number of hours community service, working with groups on programmes that address the issue of offending, working in probation and bail hostels and assisting probation officers in court work. No specific qualifications are required, but special skills can be very relevant to community service and tackling offending programmes. Experience of life and the ability to relate well make this suitable for older people.

Social worker
A field social worker has a case-load of clients with particular needs (eg children at risk, young people in trouble with the law, the physically or mentally disabled etc) and works with them to help overcome difficulties. There is a two-year training course for graduates or non-graduates leading to a professional qualification (Diploma in Social Work). Formal entry qualifications for the training course are not essential but evidence of ability to cope with the level of the course is required. Social work provides opportunities for older people with genuine commitment.

A residential social worker cares for people in residential homes for children, the disabled etc.

For further information, contact:

> Central Council for Education and Training in Social Work
> CCETSW Information Service
> St Chad's Street
> London WC1H 8AD
> 071-278 2455

Social work assistant
Opportunities for social work assistants exist both in the community and in hospitals. Assistants work alongside social workers, visiting the elderly, the disabled, families in difficulties etc, but do not take major decisions. No specific qualifications are needed, but good experience of life, a mature approach, the desire to work with people in difficulties and the ability to avoid becoming too involved are welcomed. Further information can be obtained from your local Social Services Department.

Warden of sheltered accommodation

There is no upper age limit. The warden is responsible for the welfare of residents, which involves visiting them daily, shopping, arranging social events etc. A house or flat goes with the post. No specific qualifications are required but previous experience of work with the elderly is an advantage. Further information can be obtained from your local Housing Department.

Teaching/Training/Guidance

Jobs in this category call for:

- an interest in people
- the confidence to be in charge of groups or classes
- good communication, both written and spoken
- good organisational skills
- a sound knowledge of a particular subject
- enthusiasm

Careers officer

Careers officers help young people and adults make choices about training courses and careers. The work involves interviewing clients, group work and liaising with schools and colleges. A one-year training course leads to the Diploma in Careers Guidance. Most applicants for the course have a degree; however, older applicants without a degree but with good industrial or commercial experience are also considered. Further information is obtainable from:

> Institute of Careers Officers
> 27a Lower High Street
> Stourbridge
> West Midlands BY8 1TA

Consultant/interviewer with private employment agency

Duties are to interview job-seekers and arrange interviews with prospective employers. This may involve giving guidance to enable realistic decisions to be taken. Consultants also take down

Job Opportunities

information about vacancies from employers. There are no specific entry requirements, but you need to be adaptable, understanding, perceptive and able to work under pressure.

Driving instructor
Most instructors start by working for a driving school and later become self-employed. They need to be interested in people and teaching, as well as in cars and driving, and should possess patience and a calm temperament. You must pass the Department of Transport's written and practical examinations to become a registered instructor. Some firms have an upper age limit for entry of 45. Further information is available from:

> Department of Transport, DDT3
> 2 Marsham Street
> London SW1P 3EB
> 071-212 3434

Driving examiner
Examiners must have had a driving licence for six years without a serious motoring conviction and extensive experience of driving a range of vehicles. Entrance is by examination, interview and driving test. Details are available from the Department of Transport (address above).

Placement officer with training organisation
Training organisations running youth training or training for adults (see Chapter 10) require placement officers to find suitable work placements for trainees. The work involves liaising with employers and monitoring trainees' progress; dealing with problems that may arise; paperwork. No specific qualifications are required but good organisational skills, the ability to get on well with people and to be understanding yet firm are an advantage. Further information is available from local training organisations (addresses from your local Jobcentre).

Training officer with training organisation
Training organisations require training officers to undertake a wide range of training from particular crafts taught in training

workshops to assessment courses, health and safety courses etc. A teaching qualification is not normally required for these posts. Further information can be obtained from training organisations (addresses from your local Jobcentre).

Teacher
Opportunities exist for older people to enter the teaching profession. Mature people with qualifications less than the minimum or others with vocational qualifications and relevant work experience may be considered for degree courses leading to Qualified Teacher Status (QTS). The articled Teacher Scheme is an alternative method of training, normally requiring a degree or equivalent for entry. Articled teachers learn 'on the job' during a two-year period and are paid a special bursary rather than a grant. There is currently a shortage of teachers in maths, physics, technology, CDT, chemistry, modern languages, Welsh and combined/balanced science. Teachers must be able to plan work, control classes and motivate pupils. There are some opportunities for teaching or coaching outside schools, eg in hospitals, prisons, at home.

Further information is available from your local authority and:

Department for Education
Elizabeth House
39 York Road
London SE1 7PH
071-925 5000

Lecturer in college of further education or Adult Education Centre
Opportunities exist for part-time or full-time lecturers for a wide range of courses, both academic and non-academic, eg secretarial, plumbing, brickwork, woodwork, nursery nursing etc and many leisure interests courses. Teaching qualifications are preferable but not essential. Full-time and part-time one-year training courses are available. For further information, contact the Department of Education and Science (address above) or your local college.

Tutor for Open Learning courses
There are opportunities for people to tutor students following Open Learning courses through the Open College or a training organisation. This is usually on a one-to-one basis, through arranged meetings, telephone contact or correspondence.

Further information is available from your local Open College Centre and training organisations (colleges of further education will tend to use their own staff for tutoring).

Ancillary helper
Opportunities are increasing for assistants to help with disabled children integrated into junior and secondary schools. Teaching qualifications are not required but patience, understanding and the ability to work as one of a team are essential.

Further information can be obtained from your local education authority.

Sales

To be suited to a job in this category you will probably be:

- outgoing
- good at expressing yourself
- good with figures
- enthusiastic
- tactful

Market research
Some opportunities exist for part-time interviewers doing field work. You will usually need a car. Surveys are carried out by companies and the government's Social Survey Division.

Sales assistant
This has been a difficult area for older people but the trend is changing. Supermarkets are looking for older employees; so are shops where advice is given or specialist knowledge needed, eg wallpaper and print shops, leisure buildings, retailers of furniture, soft furnishings, antiques.

Sales assistant in garden centre
Assistants should have an interest in gardening and preferably be reasonably knowledgeable (and prepared to learn!). They must enjoy helping customers and discussing purchases with them. Weekend work is involved, probably on a rota basis.

Sales representative (including insurance sales)
You need to be able to work on your own and may spend a great deal of time travelling and away from home. Some sales representatives have previous retailing experience but others have quite different backgrounds.

For further information, contact:

>Institute of Sales and Marketing Management
>Georgian House
>31 Upper George Street
>Luton
>Bedfordshire LU1 2RD
>0582 411136

Security and protective services, law and order

For this work you need to be:

- confident
- firm and authoritative when necessary
- calm in difficult situations
- quick thinking
- able to communicate well
- able to produce good character references

Court usher
The usher helps to run the court. He checks the arrivals of defendants and witnesses, and instructs people how to take the oath. The work may involve clerical duties when the court is not sitting and is particularly suitable for older people. Further information is obtainable from the local Magistrates' Clerk's Office.

Job Opportunities

Prison officer
The work involves general surveillance duties in prisons as well as escorting prisoners to and from court and to other penal establishments. Opportunities also exist for specialist trades officers to work as instructors in workshops. They must be patient, resilient, flexible and prepared to work in difficult conditions. No formal qualifications are required but there is a pre-entry test and selection interview. The upper age limit is normally 49. Applicants must be 5ft 6in or over (women 5ft 3in or over) and in good general health.

Further information is obtainable from:

> Home Office
> Cleland House
> Page Street
> London SW1P 4WN

Traffic warden
The work involves traffic control in an allocated area. Wardens patrol the streets on foot looking out for parking offences, supervising busy road crossings, doing point duty etc. They must be able to deal with the public and handle difficult situations. The job is very suitable for fit older people. There may be an upper age limit of 59 in some areas. Further information is available from regional Police Headquarters.

Security officer
Security officers protect people and property. They may be based on one site or responsible for several sites. Some security officers travel in armoured vans, collecting and delivering valuables; others patrol and inspect sites. The work is particularly suitable for ex-policemen, fire servicemen and servicemen/women, who must be physically fit and have excellent character references.

Case studies
When **Barbara** had to leave what had been her home for the last ten years and move to a new town because of her husband's job, she was very apprehensive about starting again. With her fiftieth birthday

approaching, she felt that getting a new job would be almost impossible and that it was far too late to make new friends.

Six months later she was working in a soft furnishing shop, a far cry from anything she had done before, and enjoying the challenge. She had always been interested in materials and furnishings, though she had never had much time for sewing herself. Her previous job in the Tourist Information Centre had given her plenty of experience in dealing with all sorts of people in all sorts of situations and the easy, helpful manner she had developed was ideal for working in a shop where customers wanted advice, time to make up their minds and often someone else's opinion. This had come over clearly at the interview and had been a major factor towards her being offered the job. She had also been prepared to work on Saturdays, always one of the busiest days.

Barbara admits that she applied unsuccessfully for several jobs before getting this one. She feels that this was the most suitable for an older person because it involves giving help and advice and the customers appreciate her mature approach. Always happier working than staying at home, Barbara settled into a new town very much more quickly than she imagined.

The engineering firm that had employed **Martin** for 22 years made him redundant when he was 49. After working successfully in sales and marketing for so many years his redundancy came as a bombshell and it took him several months to get to grips with the situation. At first he felt he had lost everything as his whole life style, including most of his friends, had been linked so closely to his job, and he could see no future.

Gradually, he emerged from this state and started to look out for jobs in sales and marketing. One interview followed another but nothing came of them. Looking back now he wishes that he had had some guidance at this stage to help him see that many of the skills he had developed could be used in other fields.

His break came when he applied for a job as a training officer with a training organisation that runs courses for the unemployed. He had done some staff training in his previous job but it was only when this job came along that he realised this was something he could build up and develop further instead of concentrating on sales and marketing.

When he was appointed, he began to feel himself become a complete person again. His self-respect was gradually restored and he started to make new friends among his colleagues. There were difficulties to overcome, he admits. For the first few months he worried about making the grade and keeping the job. He desperately wanted reassurance that he was 'doing all right' and nobody actually put this into words. He found it difficult at first to organise the paperwork as previously that had always been done by a secretary, but he learnt!

In fact, Martin was doing well. He brought to the job valuable experience of industry and employers, an open mind and a determination to succeed. He became one of a team very quickly and, like the others, found that his job satisfaction lay in his ability to help people. His work made him much more aware of the struggles and problems other people have and this made him, as a person, more understanding. The experience of being made redundant almost broke him, but now that is behind him he is glad to have had the chance to change direction.

Robert was 51 when he started to look for another job. For 30 years he had worked in the traffic department of the Police Force spending much of his time on car patrol and giving evidence in the magistrates' courts. He knew he would probably have to retire at 55 and he felt it would be more difficult to find work then. Over the years he had become familiar with court procedure and found it interesting, so when he saw a vacancy for a court usher advertised he applied and was appointed.

It was quite a contrast to be working indoors all day after so many years of police patrol in a rural area but he did not find it too difficult to adjust. He describes the job as assisting in the smooth running of the court. This includes helping defendants and witnesses when they arrive and maintaining a calm atmosphere in the waiting-room. Some situations needed very careful handling. Most days Robert spends time in the court room listening to cases as he waits to bring in defendants and witnesses. There is a lighter side to the job which became evident when he recounted some of the weird and wonderful excuses given by people in the dock! However, on occasions, cases can become very boring and repetitive and it can be difficult to keep awake. Back in the magistrates' clerk's office there are a number of jobs for Robert to do before court starts in the morning and at the end of the day.

Robert enjoys the job. He sees the waiting-room as similar in some aspects to the waiting-room of a doctor's surgery! His previous experience has been helpful but he feels that it is a job that does not require any particular background. Common sense and the ability to get on with all sorts of people and gain their respect are the qualities most needed. In his opinion, it is definitely a job for an older person.

Further information and help

These books should be available in your library or careers office:

Occupations (COIC). A detailed occupation guide with information on late entry to many of the jobs.

Job Ideas (COIC). 729 job titles classified by the type of activity and the level of qualification or experience involved in the jobs.

What Else Can You Do? (COIC). A guide to change and career planning for adults.

What Can a Teacher Do Except Teach? (COIC)

What Can a Nurse Do? (COIC)

Agencies and other organisations

Age Concern. Age Concern runs employment bureaux for people over 60 in certain areas. Mainly unskilled part-time work. Contact local Age Concern group (See telephone directory).

Part-time Careers Ltd, 10 Golden Square, London W1R 3AF. Specialises in part-time secretarial jobs as well as accountancy, bookkeeping and similar work.

Royal British Legion Attendants Co Ltd, 2A Rathmore Road, Charlton, London SE7 7QW. Offers full- or part-time work for ex-servicemen and women. Typical jobs are security officers, commissionaires, etc.

Success after 60. 40-41 Old Bond Street, London W1X 3AF. Caters for people from age of 50.

CHAPTER 6
Self-Employment

Having what it takes

Courage, determination and a good idea make a launch pad for starting your own business. Not everyone is lucky enough to have a sound idea when they first start thinking about self-employment, but ideas can be generated. Courage and determination, however, have to be there from the beginning.

The attractions of self-employment are plentiful, particularly for anyone who has spent many years working for other people and at the mercy of the decisions of others. Being your own boss, working on a business project you really believe in and enjoy, possibly working from home, reaping the financial reward of your hard work: this presents an exciting challenge. The government is encouraging the setting up of small businesses by making financial help available and by their praise and support of initiative and independence. In many ways, the economic and political climate is right for self-employment.

The attractions must, however, be balanced against the hazards. There are bound to be set-backs, difficult decisions, cash flow problems and financial risks, and anyone who lacks confidence or tends to be over-anxious should not pursue this option. It is worth asking yourself honestly if you have these qualities and skills:

- *Stamina.* You may find yourself working harder than you have ever done before
- *Commitment.* A belief in your goal is essential

- *The ability to organise your time.* This can be more difficult if you are working from home
- *The ability to communicate with others.* This is essential for marketing your product or service
- *The ability to make decisions and to take calculated risks when necessary*
- *Common sense*
- *A willingness to ask for help and advice*

Running your own business can be a strain not only for you but for your family too. Make sure you have their support and understanding. Without it, life could become very difficult.

Generating ideas

If you do not have a definite business idea in mind, it does not necessarily mean that self-employment is not for you. Ideas can be generated in several ways.

Identifying a particular need in your area can be a starting point. It was lack of certain provision in a particular community that led Helen Lewis to start her business.

Case study

Helen Lewis was made redundant when she was 50. She had worked in a bakery in a small town for 20 years and when it was closed down she was faced with the prospect of never finding another job. She had no experience outside the bakery and the unemployment rate in the area was high. One thing she was sure of was that she did not want to retire. This led her to think about self-employment.

There was no laundry service or launderette in the town and she had felt for some time that there was a need for one, particularly in view of the increasing number of people coming into the area to retire because of the low cost of housing. With these people in mind she planned to offer the option of a collection and delivery service and an ironing service. She carried out a survey to gauge the interest of her potential customers and found the response encouraging. She went on to seek professional advice through the business and enterprise services and made a successful application for an Enterprise Allowance. This, together with her redundancy payment, helped her get started.

Self-Employment

Helen's biggest problem was finding suitable premises to rent, but she now has a good central position. She is working extremely hard to build up the business but is enjoying the challenge and the sense of purpose it has given her.

Another way of generating ideas is to think of all the small businesses that you can and then consider whether any of them could be copied or adapted. There could be a danger of over-provision if you started a business similar to an existing one in the same area. On the other hand, competition can be good.

Many people have developed specific skills at work or in their leisure time and sometimes these can lead to business ideas. For example, someone who has always enjoyed cooking might consider catering for parties in people's homes; someone who has always enjoyed spending much of his free time being the family's car mechanic could adapt his mechanical skills to the service and repair of garden machinery.

Being self-employed does not necessarily mean starting a completely new business. If you have sufficient capital, whether it be savings or a redundancy settlement, you might decide to buy and carry on running an existing business. Another possibility is franchising, where you buy the right to sell someone else's idea.

Any list of ideas is bound to be limited, but it can help to look at some possibilities which do not all involve great capital outlay:

- building repairs
- painting and decorating
- electrical work
- garden landscaping
- garden/grounds maintenance
- growing plants/vegetables for sale
- car repairs and servicing at customer's house
- upholstery
- French polishing
- dressmaking
- clothes repairs and alterations
- home-based office services
- driving instructor
- taxi service
- photography
- videos for special occasions
- picture-framing
- freelance writing
- coaching for exams/agency
- running a pub
- running a sub-post office
- sales agent
- running a shop
- market stall

craft work, eg wood turning, glass engraving, soft toys, jewellery
child minding
running a home for the elderly
mobile hairdressing service
agency for cleaning and gardening services
boarding kennels
catering for functions
bed and breakfast

Taking all the responsibility or sharing it

When you start running your own business you may want to carry all the responsibility for it, in which case you will be a sole trader, or you may want to share the responsibility by forming a partnership. Alternatively, you might decide to take up a franchise.

As a *sole trader* you may work on your own or employ other people, but you will be in control of the business. You will have all the profits but you are also responsible for any debts that are incurred. If things went badly wrong and you went bankrupt, your creditors could seize your personal possessions as well as your business assets. You do not have to register your business, but everyone starting a business has to notify the Inland Revenue and the Department of Social Security.

A *partnership* consists of two or more people who share the responsibility, the profits and the risks. They will be personally liable for debts. Although it is not essential, it is advisable to have a legally drawn-up partnership agreement. So often, partners fall out with each other. Some people say that choosing a partner in business is as difficult and important as choosing a wife or husband.

If you join a *cooperative* you will not be self-employed, but there are so many similarities between a cooperative and a small business that it is important to mention this as an option. Cooperatives are collectively owned by the people who work in them and the responsibilities and profits are shared by the whole team. Cooperatives have limited liability so that individual members are not personally liable for debts in the case of bankruptcy.

Franchising is described by the British Franchise Association as 'the method by which the owner of a business (franchisor) contractually agrees to allow another independent person or company (franchisee) to market its products or service within a specified geographical area. In return the franchisee pays an initial fee for the rights to the area and a royalty on sales giving the franchisor a percentage benefit on sales'. The advantages are that you are selling a product or service that has already proved itself and is usually nationally known; you have the support and advice of the franchisor; you will probably be given training. However, you are not completely independent and it is important to take legal advice before entering into a contract. It has been said that starting your own business can be like walking alone in the jungle. If you start by taking a franchise you have a knowledgeable hunter at your side.

Testing the market

It may be necessary to test the viability of more than one idea before making any firm commitment. This will involve carrying out some market research to find out what demand there is for your product or service.

Start by trying to identify your potential customers who will all have certain things in common, for example:

- They must be able to afford your product or service
- They must have a need for your product or service or be likely to find it an attractive, interesting or useful proposition
- They should be prepared to give your product or service a chance
- They may have to live within a reasonable distance of your base

Once you have done this, select a sample of your potential customers and try to find out their reaction to your business proposal. How you do this will depend very much on the nature of the business, but you could try any of these methods:

- *Using a questionnaire.* This is likely to work best if you fill it in with the potential customer rather than relying on him to

complete it and return it at some later date. Questions should aim to find out the prices you can charge, how often your services are likely to be used, what the customer's needs are, whether he is committed to another supplier, what the potential customer feels generally about your proposal.
- *Calling on people* to sound out their reactions in more general terms
- Carefully planned *telephone enquiries*
- *Using local authority marketing and research services* where available. This is more appropriate for the larger business venture. The authority may be able to supply a list of company names and addresses, information on products, turnover, number of employees etc
- *Consulting the local chamber of commerce*

This can be a difficult task and it might be tempting to rely on assumptions. Resist the temptation. The information you collect at this stage is of the greatest importance.

Look, too, at your competition. Once you have identified it, try to analyse its strengths and weaknesses so that you can see more clearly where you might be able to gain an advantage. If there is no competition there may be no demand for your product or service!

Drawing up a business plan

You will be spending much of your time working out how to finance your business. The initial outlay on premises and equipment must be calculated as well as the necessary working capital. If you need to borrow money you will probably have to provide your bank manager with a *cash flow forecast*. This is a document explaining what you expect to have to spend each month and what your estimated monthly takings will be. You may have to take into account the length of credit you can obtain from your suppliers and whether or not the goods or services will be sold on a cash basis or whether you are going to offer credit facilities to your customers. It is very important to take specialist advice on the best way to draw this up.

The cash flow forecast will be central to your overall business

Self-Employment

plan, which should also include details of your product and its manufacture or your service, premises and equipment, marketing proposals and methods of promotion. You may decide to draw up a five-year plan initially and then a more detailed plan for the first 12 months. A good business plan is the result of thorough research. It can go a long way towards convincing a bank manager that you will succeed!

Many organisations offer free professional advice to anyone planning to start their own business. Make use of all the help there is and find out as much as you can about financial assistance. The advisers are well-informed and experienced businessmen and can help in many ways including:

- providing information about grants, loans, government schemes
- helping to draw up a cash flow forecast and a business plan
- assessing whether your plans are economically sound
- explaining the different legal implications of being a sole trader, entering into a partnership, or becoming a limited company
- discussing premises and planning permission (this is often required if your business is run from home)
- referring you to an accountant, solicitor, insurance agent
- discussing tax and VAT
- providing information about training courses

Organisations offering advice

Local Enterprise Agencies. These agencies are usually funded by a combination of local government, central government, chambers of commerce and local businesses. They are set up to give advice on any aspect of self-employment and advise on grants and loans available from the local authority and other sources of financial support. They may be able to give practical help in finding suitable premises. Contact your local authority, or dial 100 and ask for Freefone Enterprise or write to Business in the Community at 227a City Road, London ECW 1LX, or Romano House, 43 Station Road, Edinburgh E12 7AF.

Business and enterprise services. The Training and Enterprise Council (TEC) in your area provides help for people who want to start their own business. They offer:
- free counselling and advice
- courses in business management to help you set up your business and later on to expand or develop
- Enterprise Allowance until your business starts to bring in a regular income. The amount and period of financial help are decided locally. (This replaces the Enterprise Allowance Scheme.)

Find out about these types of business and enterprise services at your local TEC or Jobcentre. They may have their own local names but the same range of services will be on offer.

Small Firms Service. This service is run by the Department of Employment and offers advice and information. The information service is free and so are the first three advice counselling sessions; after that there is a charge. The Service produces very good leaflets including: 'Starting Your Own Business', 'Running Your Own Business', 'Marketing', 'Franchising', 'Trade Credit' etc. Contact them by dialling 100 and asking for Freefone Enterprise.

The Rural Development Commission. The Commission offers advice and training to anyone wanting to start or expand a business in an English rural area (apart from businesses relating to agriculture or horticulture). They can help find premises, may be able to provide loans or grants and offer a wide range of training. Contact your local Rural Development Commission office in the phone book or write to The Rural Development Commission, 141 Castle Street, Salisbury, Wiltshire SP1 3TP. A similar service is offered in Scotland and Wales by: The Scottish Development Agency, Rosebery House, Haymarket Terrace, Edinburgh EH12 5EZ and The Welsh Development Agency, Pearl House, Greyfriars Road, Cardiff CF1 3XX respectively.

Tourist Boards. They offer advice on the development of businesses related to tourism. Grants can be made available.

Self-Employment

British Steel Corporation. They offer advice and financial support to anyone starting a new business where steel industry jobs have been lost. Further information through the Local Enterprise Agency or by contacting BSC (Industry) Ltd, 12 Addiscombe Road, Croydon CR4 2LJ.

British Coal Enterprise Ltd. They offer financial help and assistance with premises for businesses setting up in traditional coal-mining areas and creating jobs. Information through the Local Enterprise Agency or contact British Coal Enterprise Ltd, 14–15 Lower Grosvenor Place, London SW1W 0EX.

Banks. Most banks offer free expert advice. They may be able to offer you a loan or arrange an overdraft facility. Basic banking services are free for 12 months for anyone on an Enterprise Allowance scheme.

Accountants. Your Local Enterprise Agency will be able to put you in touch with an accountant.

The British Franchise Association. The Association produces a number of publications on franchising including a Franchise Information Pack. They offer help and advice to franchisees and franchisors. Their address is:

>Thames View
>Newtown Road
>Henley-on-Thames
>Oxfordshire RG9 1HG

Training

It is advisable to make use of the training courses available in business skills unless you have already had good experience of the financial management of a business. You are taking an unnecessary risk if you decide to learn by your mistakes!

The courses in business management funded by the TECs are run at colleges of further education or training centres and are usually free of charge.

Many private training agencies run courses which are usually well advertised in local newspapers.

The Open College runs courses for people starting in business. These courses can be studied at home with back-up support from a tutor at the Open College centre. Contact your local college of further education for information about Open College and other Open Learning courses.

Case studies

Not all businesses succeed but many do. These case studies describe the setting up of four businesses, some of the problems encountered and the satisfactions gained.

When **Tom** resigned from his job in the plastics industry he decided to retire to a bungalow in the south of England. It was not long before he realised that at 58 he was certainly not ready for retirement and when someone commented that he was living in 'God's waiting-room' he decided enough was enough. He moved north and found a small inexpensive unit in a converted mill and started a wood-turning business.

With the help of the Enterprise Allowance he began manufacturing a range of products, including wooden lamp stands, clocks, bowls, wheelbarrows etc. When he reached the point where he was making more than he was selling he decided to open a small shop in partnership with a glass engraver. In fact, this took up a considerable amount of the time he would rather have spent making his goods. Talking now, a couple of years later, Tom says that selling was the area in which he most needed help and advice. His real break came when he started to make promotional items for companies. This part of the business, in particular, has grown rapidly and he has now established a name for himself. He took on another wood turner who has now become a partner and the business has gone from strength to strength.

When Tom started he got in touch with the Rural Development Commission who he has found very helpful. As well as giving advice they have brought him business, as he is now teaching woodturning to the Commission's woodworking instructors. Tom's business has the capacity to develop in several directions. He finds it challenging and exciting and is full of ideas for the future.

Self-Employment

Pat Griffiths decided that she wanted to work for herself, spend more time in her own home and become more involved in the local community. It was family circumstances that were instrumental in her change of career.

Pat was 45 when she decided to give up her job as a secretary to spend more time helping her mother when she had a stroke. Pat felt very close to her mother who had been a great support to her when she was left to bring up two small children on her own. She wanted to help her fulfil her wish of staying in her own home for as long as possible and knew that this would involve a great deal of time. Five years later her mother died. By now Pat's children had left home and she was on her own in a three-bedroomed house.

After a gap of five years Pat felt very apprehensive about returning to secretarial work. She had never used a word processor or a computer and she did not want to go on a course to update her skills. More important than that, she did not want to go back to a nine-to-five job, returning each evening to an empty house. She really wanted to work for herself and spend more time in her own home.

Pat had enjoyed looking after her mother, though it had meant she felt she was living in two houses at once. She had a good understanding of the needs of the elderly and a naturally caring personality. She decided to contact the Social Services Department to find out about the Boarding Out for the Elderly Scheme. This allows a person to take up to three people without having to be registered as a home by the local authority. The financial arrangements made it a viable proposition and Pat decided to go ahead with it.

Pat finds this way of life very fulfilling. As a secretary she had to be efficient and have good organisational skills. She certainly needs these now. She enjoys creating a homely, cheerful atmosphere for her elderly people and is glad to have her house fully used. She has become more involved in the local community, something she always regretted not being able to do when she was working in a nine-to-five job.

Jo is now running his own saddlery business, something he would never have dreamt he would be doing ten years ago. His last job as a transport and warehouse manager seems to have little connection on the face of it, and yet the strong hands and manual dexterity needed for any mechanical work are also needed for saddlery.

How did it happen? Well, Jo was made redundant and suddenly had a lot of time on his hands. He also had a back problem, probably caused by his work as a mechanic in his early days. It was because of this that he was registered disabled. The future looked bleak and to pass the time Jo used to go along to some riding stables owned by a friend and help out. The tack had pretty hard use and much of it needed repairing so there was always something to do. It soon became evident that Jo was very good at repairing tack and the idea began to develop. Everyone said that saddlery was a dying art and both his friend and his wife urged him to see if he could go on a course to learn the trade before setting up on his own.

Jo went along to the Jobcentre and was told that if he could find someone to train him the Local Training and Enterprise Council would pay for it because he was disabled. Finding someone was the first problem! It looked a hopeless situation, but eventually Jo found a saddler running a one-man business who was prepared to take him on. The saddler he trained with was a real master of his trade with a great reputation. He was not the easiest person to work with but he helped Jo to cover four years' work in one, so that by the end he was ready to start out on his own.

During the first year, Jo received the Enterprise Allowance. By the end of this year, business was increasing but he needed to invest in more tools and equipment. He says he could have done with the allowance for a bit longer. The Development Commission gave him advice and encouragement and he is still in contact with them. The business is now in its second year and Jo is pleased with the progress he is making. 'When you're on the dole', he said, 'you're not living, just existing.'

Any advice for others? Jo talked about needing to be 'a bit bull-headed' to overcome the obstacles and at the same time 'laid back' – not suitable, he said, for a 'middle-aged worrier'!

Elaine left her job as an office supervisor with a finance company after a disagreement with her boss. She had been very pressurised and when she left she felt a mixture of relief and apprehension. She registered as unemployed, but did not receive benefit for the first few weeks because she had left the job of her own accord.

Instead of going back into full-time employment, she decided that she would like to develop her hobby into a business, so she made enquiries about the Enterprise Allowance and took up the offer of free business advice and counselling. She was disconcerted to be told not to turn her hobby into a business, but was not put off! She

Self-Employment

planned to make and sell cross-stitch pictures, trinket boxes etc; to run evening classes and give talks and demonstrations to promote her work.

Elaine knew that there was a demand for her work and for teaching as friends had been asking her to make pictures for special presents for some time and she had often been asked to give lessons. She also knew that she would never make a fortune out of her business, but as her husband was in full-time employment she would not be totally dependent on it: it would be a useful second income.

It is now nine months since Elaine started and she talked about some of the early difficulties. First and foremost was the danger of becoming over-committed and making life as stressful as it was before! She is learning to control incoming orders and to pace her work better. She has had to learn the hard way to look at orders from an economic angle rather than from a desire to please customers. Another difficulty has been getting the balance right between time spent producing pictures and marketing them.

In spite of the difficulties, Elaine has no regrets about the decision she took. She loves the work and is particularly enthusiastic about teaching. She enjoys seeing other people mastering the art that she finds immensely rewarding and she definitely enjoys being her own boss.

Further information and help

Your local library should have a selection of books on self-employment. Look out for:

Working for Yourself, 13th edition, Godfrey Golzen (Kogan Page)

Going Freelance, 3rd edition, Godfrey Golzen (Kogan Page)

Starting a Successful Small Business, 2nd edition, M J Morris (Kogan Page)

Be Your Own Boss – Starter Kit, D S Watkins (National Extension College)

Starting Your Own Business, (The Consumers' Association) How to make a success of going it alone.

How to Prepare a Business Plan, Edward Blackwell (Kogan Page)

Taking Up a Franchise: The Daily Telegraph Guide, 9th edition, Colin Barrow and Godfrey Golzen (Kogan Page)

Directory of Franchising (Franchising Publications)

A full list of Kogan Page titles on self-employment and small businesses is available from the publisher.

CHAPTER 7
Part-Time Work

Why part time?

According to a Labour Force Survey of the workforce in employment in Britain, the increase in the number of part-time jobs is considerably higher than the increase in full-time jobs. Full-time work is taken to be 31 or more hours a week and part-time 30 hours or less.

The reason for this continuing growth must be that part-time work often suits employer and employee better than full-time. From the employer's point of view, part-time work offers much more flexibility. He is able to vary the number of staff to meet the demands at certain times of the day or year. Take, for example, the hotel and catering trade. Part-time staff are brought in when the work peaks to supplement full-time staff. The retail trade, too, is employing more part-time staff to cover the busy times of the day which avoids having people standing idle during the slack times. This is bound to be more cost effective than employing all full-time staff.

Many employers find that part-time staff are particularly reliable and well motivated. They are often prepared to stay longer to finish a job when necessary without counting up the minutes of overtime. On the whole, older people working part time are not under such pressure outside work and this can have a marked impact on attitudes and energy. They often value the social contact that work brings as a refreshing change from home. This can, of course, apply to full-time staff too, but perhaps they tend to take the relationship with colleagues more for granted.

There can be several reasons for taking a part-time job rather than a full-time job later on in your working life. Let us look at some of them:

- You want to trade in part of your current income for more free time
- You want a part-time job because you feel it would be less stressful
- You want to give out-of-work activities and interests greater priority
- You want to combine two or three part-time jobs to give greater variety
- You can use part-time work as a way of improving your chances of getting back into full-time work
- There are health reasons which make part-time work a more realistic option
- There is no alternative at a particular time

Whatever your reasons, part-time work could be the answer you are looking for. It could lead to a better balanced life-style and open up other opportunities.

The disadvantages

Consider the disadvantages too, though. It takes time to adapt to a part-time job if you have been used to full-time work. To begin with, you feel a bit of an outsider. Not being 'there' all the time means that you have to update yourself continually with what has been happening. There may be some staff you rarely see because they are part time too and come on different days.

Some part-time staff feel that they are being taken advantage of. It sometimes seems to them that they are doing far more work in proportion to their hours than colleagues – they may even feel they are doing a full-time job in half the normal hours. They are not given the status they would like in the workplace and do not feel as secure.

With any luck, these problems, if they do exist, can be overcome gradually. This will depend on you, the part-timer, as well as your colleagues. Tact and understanding can solve most things as can an awareness of what the difficulties are. A full-time member of staff might, for example, resent a part-timer's shorter hours and relative freedom – overlooking the fact that this is balanced out in the pay packet.

Different forms of part-time work

The term 'flexible working' is now used to cover the different forms of part-time work as well as some full-time working arrangements. Flexible working means working in a way that differs from the normal full-time pattern (for example a 9–5 day or a five-day week).

1. Permanent part-time work

Some part-time jobs involve working for a few hours each day; others for a couple of days or more a week. Some jobs are part time because they never occupy anyone for more than a short time each day or week, for example school dinner helpers, school crossing attendants; the majority, however, cover almost as wide a range as full-time jobs, for example nursing, teaching auxiliary, office work, retail.

Part-time work on a permanent basis gives a good basic structure to the week, unlike temporary or seasonal work which requires a much more flexible approach.

Mary Hunt has found that part-time work suits her very well.

Case study

Ten years ago, **Mary** and her husband David gave up their respective jobs and took over the running of a country pub. This had been their ambition for many years and they both enjoyed the challenge it offered. They built up the trade steadily to begin with and developed the bar meals. During the last couple of years, business has not been going so well. Another pub in the village has been given a major face-lift and drawn away some of their customers. Both Mary and David feel, too, that changing attitudes to drink/driving affected them badly. People are no longer so prepared to drive out to a country pub for a drink when they can walk to a pub in town. The work became a struggle and regretfully they decided that they must give up.

Mary no longer wanted to be so heavily committed and she decided to look for part-time work. The job she found was connected with the Home Help Service and is called an Evening Care Assistant. It involves visiting her clients in their homes in the evening and helping them get ready for bed.

Some need help washing and undressing while others just need a friendly chat and the knowledge that someone is coming along to make sure they are all right. She checks that the doors are locked and everything is safe. If there are any problems, she contacts the doctor or social worker.

Mary works up to 15 hours a week, five nights a week from Mondays to Fridays. She is paid on an hourly rate but her hours are not always regular and sometimes her numbers drop for a week or two. Because of this, Mary feels it could never be more than a supplementary income.

Applicants had to have their own car but there were no specific requirements for the job by way of qualifications. Mary comes over as a very caring and responsible person. She nursed her own elderly parents for several years and she felt that this was seen to be important at her interview. She had to pass a medical examination and said too that her background was checked. She was over 50 when she applied for the job and she felt that her age had been no barrier.

Mary finds the job very rewarding. Her clients are always waiting for her to come in the evening and she knows her visits put their minds at rest. She feels close to them and likes to do a little bit for them over and above her duties. Evening work suits her very well as she likes to be at home during the day.

There are a few snags. The link with the social worker is not always easy, as the social worker may not know the whole situation. Bad winter weather can make night driving difficult and Mary never likes letting her clients down.

The disadvantages are outweighed by the enjoyment Mary gets from the contact with people who need her. She spoke enthusiastically and warmly about her work. It is very different from any paid work she has done before, but is using her particular strengths and skills.

2. Job sharing

Job sharing is a term used to describe two or more employees combining to do one full-time job. It aims to protect the status and promotion prospects of employees, both of which are at risk with part-time employment. Some employers advertise posts as suitable for one full-time person or for job sharing. In such a situation, two people applying to job share have to present a very convincing case. Preparing for an interview always takes time but if you are applying to job share you need to think through the situation in detail. It helps if you know your sharer well as it is essential that you work as a team. An older person working with a younger person can be a good combination as the older person is able to help out in emergencies, when children are sick and in school holidays. A good job-sharing partnership can bring many benefits to an employer. In theory, there should never be any break in the continuity of the post. This means that good communication with your job-share partner is essential! Many of the job-sharing posts are to be found in the public sector and include teaching, clerical work, reception work, librarian assistant. It is not always necessary to find your own partner.

3. Temporary work

Temporary work, or 'temping' as it is called when it is office work, requires an adaptable and unflustered approach: you are always being put into new situations and having new demands made of you. It can provide an opportunity for getting back into work and can, not infrequently, lead to the offer of a permanent, full-time or part-time job. The majority of temporary work is office based, but there are also opportunities for nursing, production work, market research surveys etc.

4. Seasonal work

Seasonal work can be a useful stop-gap or for some people it might provide a work pattern that suits well for a number of years. Most seasonal work is linked to agriculture, horticulture, travel and tourism, eg holiday camps, hotel work, counter work, glass-house growing etc.

John Middleton's hours vary considerably according to the season.

Case study
   John Middleton was 55 when he found himself unemployed. John was the manager of a shoe shop which was part of a national chain in

the Midlands. He had worked for the same company for 20 years and had been manager for the last ten. He was made redundant because the shop was to be demolished to make way for a new shopping complex. The company was planning to reopen their branch once the development had been completed but this would not be for 12 months and John had been told that it was company policy now to appoint managers in their thirties.

Under John's management, the shop had built up a good reputation in the town. John was good at staff management and took great pleasure in seeing customers satisfied with his service. However, he found himself under increasing pressure from the head office. Competition in the town was becoming more of a threat and he was held responsible for any drop in turnover. He was frequently being called on to give detailed explanations of why projected targets had not been met, even though, in his opinion, the targets were often unrealistic. This had become a great strain.

In the first few weeks after being made redundant, John felt his situation was hopeless. He spent long hours working in the garden where he could think more clearly. Gardening had always been his main interest and he was very knowledgeable about it.

When John saw a job advertised for a sales assistant at a local garden centre at weekends he applied for it and was appointed. From the employer's point of view he was an ideal candidate because of his previous experience in retail, his knowledge of and interest in gardening and his flexible approach to hours of work. At first he just worked at weekends, but now he works five days a week in the busy season, two days mid-season and not at all in January and February. He is very happy with this arrangement. He has traded in status, responsibility and pressure for job satisfaction, variety and flexibility that allows time for other things.

5. Term-time working

Employees can take unpaid leave during school holidays. This is only possible in a limited number of occupations.

Employment rights for part-time employees

All employers have to observe certain rights giving essential protection to workers. The Acts that cover this basic protection are:

Part-Time Work

- The Health and Safety at Work Act. Employers are bound by law to ensure as far as possible that their employees work in a safe environment
- The Race Relations Act, the Equal Pay Act and the Sex Discrimination Act. These Acts make it illegal to discriminate on grounds of race or sex when recruiting, training, paying or promoting employees. (There are a few exceptions to these Acts)
- The Trade Union and Labour Relations Act. This protects employees from being victimised by their employers for taking part in trade union activities

Other rights do not apply equally to all employees and it is the part-time workers who fare the worst. Information and advice can be obtained from any regional office of the Advisory, Conciliation and Arbitration Service (ACAS). A few points that should be considered at this stage are:

- Anyone who works for less than eight hours a week is excluded from all but the basic rights already mentioned
- Those working for 16 hours or more will be entitled to the same rights as full-time employees provided that they meet the condition of having been in continuous employment with the same employer for a specified length of time
- Those working for over eight hours a week but under 16 hours will be eligible for the same rights as full-time employees provided that they have worked continuously for the same employer for five years

The protection rights that are most relevant for older people include:

- The right to claim unfair dismissal after working for an employer for a certain length of time
- The right to redundancy pay after being in continuous employment for two years or more (provided you are working for 16 hours or more a week, or have been working for the same employer for five years)
- The right to a written statement of your terms and conditions of employment after a certain length of time. This is not a

contract of employment but it determines that such a contract (whether it is oral or written) exists

It is important to check what your employment rights are before taking a job. It is far better to do so at this stage in order to avoid confusion and possible bad feeling later on. People working for less than eight hours a week or doing temporary/casual work must understand what their position is.

Benefits and part-time work

Earnings from part-time work can affect your entitlement to social security benefits and Housing Benefit.

1. Unemployment Benefit

If you are eligible for Unemployment Benefit and you take a part-time job you must declare it. Unemployment Benefit will only be paid to you for the days you are *not* working, unless:

- your net earnings do not exceed a set rate per day. (There are certain payments in kind or cash which are not treated as income, eg meals provided free at work)
- you are still available for work on those days

Two other conditions are:

- your earnings must come from work that is not your usual occupation
- you do not work part time on a regular basis

As long as you are claiming Unemployment Benefit you must be prepared to give up a part-time job for a full-time job. At present, anything you may earn on a Sunday is not taken into consideration as benefit is never usually paid for Sunday.

The DSS leaflet 'Voluntary and part-time workers – your benefits, pensions and National Insurance contributions' gives general guidance, but it is advisable to discuss your own situation with a claimant adviser at the Jobcentre.

The system has considerable implications for the pattern of part-time work. As it stands at the moment, it is very much more advantageous to work on one or two days a week rather than for a couple of hours each day of the week. Working for a couple of hours each day rules out all Unemployment Benefit payments and could leave you worse off.

2. Income Support and part-time work
Income Support will continue to be paid providing:

- you remain eligible for full-time work
- you work on average less than 24 hours a week

The amount you receive will be affected by the amount you earn and you will have to check your situation carefully with the Department of Social Security. A small proportion of your earnings will be disregarded in working out your entitlement. At present there are two rates, a higher figure being disregarded for people in certain circumstances, eg if you have been getting Supplementary Benefit or Income Support for two years or more.

3. Retirement pension and part-time work
The earnings limit for part-time work was abolished in autumn 1989, which means that you can earn as much as you like without your retirement pension being affected in any way.

4. Housing Benefit
If you are receiving Housing Benefit, you must inform the council that you are working part time and give them the details of your earnings, including your expenses. If you are not earning very much, your Housing Benefit will not be affected, but you must still give all the details.

National Insurance

National Insurance contributions are paid when you are working for an employer and your wage is at or above the lower earnings limit. If you are unemployed and signing on at the Jobcentre as available for full-time work you will be awarded credits instead of National Insurance contributions.

If you work part time you will still get credits provided:

- you do not earn more than a certain sum each day
- you do not work for more than eight hours a week
- if you work one day a week as an employee, your earnings that day are less than the lower earnings limit
- you are not working in your normal main occupation

If you are earning less than the lower earnings limit but your situation is not in line with the conditions under which credits are still received, you will not have to pay National Insurance contributions. However, if you do not, you will no longer be entitled to the basic benefits. It is important to consider carefully your position regarding contributions and to discuss the situation at your Social Security Office: it may be advisable to safeguard some of the benefits by paying (National Insurance) voluntary contributions. (The leaflet 'National Insurance Voluntary Contributions' gives general guidance.)

Weighing it all up

Part-time work must be an attractive option for many older people but if you are claiming benefit, you need to look at your situation very carefully. We have covered some of the major points to be considered in this chapter, but it is important to take advice from your local Social Security Department.

Further information and help

'Voluntary and part-time workers – your benefits, pensions and National Insurance contributions' (DSS). Free leaflet available in post offices, Jobcentres, Social Security Offices.

Job Sharing: A Practical Guide, Pam Walton (Kogan Page).

Part Time Careers Ltd, 10 Golden Square, London W1R 3AF. Employment agency for part-time work in London – advice and guidance given.

CHAPTER 8
Voluntary Work

Not everyone is able to find a suitable full- or part-time job in the traditional sense, nor does everyone want one. If this applies to you, you may still feel you have a lot to offer and want to become more involved in the community. Voluntary work could provide the opportunity you are looking for. Voluntary organisations form a very important part of the structure of our society providing services that would be far too costly to resource if they depended completely on government funding. Members of Relate, for example, provide a counselling service for people experiencing problems with a relationship, and in doing so supplement the work of the social services. Volunteer teachers helping adults to improve their standards of literacy and numeracy are extending adult education in the community. The magisterial system depends on people giving up their time to carry out very demanding, unpaid work in the courts, saving the tax payer a vast sum of money. Voluntary work can be just as arduous as paid work, depending on how much responsibility you take on.

What you can give and gain

You can give your time, interest and particular skills to voluntary work. The range of opportunities is far wider than most people realise. In return, you will find that you gain great satisfaction, and many of the benefits of paid employment are provided in equal measure by voluntary work. You are very unlikely to receive any payment apart from your expenses, so what exactly are these benefits? Let us consider some of them.

- *A sense of purpose.* It certainly helps to have a sense of purpose – something to concentrate on other than personal matters
- *Structure to the week.* It can be difficult to handle hours of unaccustomed free time, especially if your job has been demanding and left little opportunity for developing hobbies. The commitment that voluntary work requires, whether it be a few hours a week or a couple of days, can provide an anchor
- *Self-respect.* It is very easy to lose your self-respect temporarily when you are unemployed because your life suddenly seems so much less productive. Voluntary work brings with it a certain amount of responsibility and this restores a feeling of usefulness and self-respect. You have a position again in a team and others are dependent on you.
- *Colleagues, friends.* Colleagues and friends at work play a very important part in life and when you no longer meet them on a regular basis there is a large gap. It is never quite the same meeting for a drink or going out for a meal; the bond seems to be looser because you are no longer working together. Voluntary work brings with it new colleagues and friends as well as frequently bringing you into contact with the client group for whom you are working
- *The respect of others.* People do see you in a different light if you are prepared to become more actively involved in the community. It can certainly help family relationships at a time when they often become tense

What skills can you offer?

If you have not been involved in voluntary work before, you may not realise how varied it can be. Fund raising for some of the major charities such as Oxfam and Save the Children may spring to mind, but you may not have thought of helping to teach an adult how to read or write with Second Chance, or laying hedges with a nature conservation group. Voluntary organisations need a whole range of skills, some of which you have and some of

Voluntary Work

which you may be prepared to learn. Which of these jobs could you do?

- *Driving*. Most areas have driving schemes run by the Social Services which coordinate the requirements of the caring organisations in the area and pay a good mileage allowance. The Ambulance Service uses volunteers to drive patients to and from hospital. The British Red Cross Society and St John Ambulance need drivers
- *Secretarial work*. Most organisations need a good secretary to deal with correspondence, take the minutes at meetings, book rooms etc
- *Administrative work*. People are needed for organising events, coordinating the work of volunteers, producing newsletters, chairing meetings etc.
- *Accountancy*. Every organisation needs a treasurer responsible for the accounts
- *Giving advice and information*, eg at a Citizens' Advice Bureau which gives impartial, confidential and informed advice on any subject
- *Counselling*. A number of organisations give support through counselling. Counselling is not usually giving advice; it is listening to people's problems without standing in judgement and helping them to resolve them themselves. Samaritans offer support through counselling to anyone feeling suicidal, despairing or under stress. Cruse works in a similar way with the bereaved. You do not have to be a skilled counsellor when you join such an organisation as you will be given very good training
- *Teaching*. Opportunities exist for teaching or training where no previous teaching experience is required, for example teaching adults to improve their reading, writing or arithmetic through Second Chance; taking a training session in first aid etc
- *Home visiting the disabled or elderly*. Other groups who need visiting include people who have been the victims of crime and are left feeling afraid and vulnerable
- *Beauty care and manicure*. The British Red Cross offers this service in hospitals and day centres

- *Sales.* Several charities run shops, eg Oxfam, Hospital League of Friends, Imperial Cancer Research Fund
- *Work with animals.* Riding for the Disabled gives disabled people the chance to gain confidence and brings them great pleasure
- *First aid.* The British Red Cross Society and St John Ambulance attend public events and give first aid to anyone who needs it
- *DIY.* There is always a need for people to do painting and decorating, maintenance jobs, gardening etc
- *Fund raising* through money-raising events, appeals, raffles
- *Public speaking.* Pressure groups need people who can put a case forcefully

You can see from this list that there is much more to voluntary work than raising money or visiting the elderly, important as both of these are.

The time it takes

Some organisations ask for a definite commitment of a certain number of days or hours a week. This is the case with Relate (Marriage Guidance) and the Citizens' Advice Bureau.

Other organisations are much more flexible. If, for example, you are in a driving scheme, you will be rung up and asked if you can do a particular job. If you are unable to, someone else will be contacted.

Do not be put off by the fear that voluntary work will take up too much of your time. The amount of time you give to the job depends on you, your other commitments and what you choose to do.

Voluntary work and benefits

1. Unemployment Benefit

If you are receiving Unemployment Benefit the amount you get will not be affected by any unpaid voluntary work that you do. The only condition is that you must remain available for work. In other words, you must be prepared to give up your voluntary work if a suitable job crops up or you must restrict it to after-work hours.

If you receive payment for your voluntary work, your benefit will not be affected provided you remain available for work and your net earnings do not exceed the amount allowable per day.

2. Income Support
If you are getting benefit because you are unemployed, unpaid voluntary work will not affect the amount you receive provided you remain available for paid work for 24 hours or more a week. (There are certain circumstances when you are not required to be available for work, eg if you are a pensioner.)

If you are paid for voluntary work the amount you receive from Income Support may be affected, depending on your net earnings.

3. Retirement pension
This will not be affected by voluntary work, paid or unpaid.

A sample of voluntary organisations

It would be impossible to list all the voluntary organisations here nor would it serve a useful purpose. The organisations that have been chosen merely represent the wide range of work available in the voluntary sector. For a comprehensive list, consult the *Voluntary Agencies Directory*, which is produced by the National Council for Voluntary Organisations and should be available at your library. You will find that many organisations have local branches in your area and can be contacted through the local council for voluntary services. The addresses given here are of the headquarters.

Group 1
These organisations offer support through counselling or advice and information.

Al-Anon Family Groups UK and Eire, 61 Great Dover Street, London SE1 4YF
   Offers help to the families of problem drinkers. **Alateen** helps teenagers (aged 12–20) who are or have been affected by an alcoholic relative.

Alcohol Recovery Project (ARP), 68 Newington Causeway, London SE1 6DF.
Provides advice, information, counselling and residential services to people with a drink problem.

Cruse – Bereavement Care, Cruse House, 126 Sheen Road, Richmond, Surrey TW9 1UR. Offers a service of counselling, advice and opportunities for social contact to all bereaved people.

National Association of Citizens' Advice Bureaux, 115–123 Pentonville Road, London N1 9LZ. Provides free, impartial and confidential advice and help through local CABs to anybody on any subject.

Relate – National Marriage Guidance, Herbert Gray College, Little Church Street, Rugby, Warwickshire CV21 3AP. Gives help and advice through counselling to people experiencing relationship problems.

Samaritans, 17 Uxbridge Road, Slough, Berkshire SL1 1SN. Gives support through counselling to people who are suicidal, despairing or under stress.

These organisations provide training for their volunteers and usually expect them, in return, to undertake to work a certain number of hours a week.

Group 2

These organisations give care and support to people who find it difficult to cope independently because of their age, health or particular circumstances.

Age Concern, 1268 London Road, London SW16 4EJ. Promotes the welfare of elderly people and those who work with the elderly.

Help the Aged, 16–18 St James's Walk, London EC1R 0BE. Aims to improve the quality of life of elderly people, particularly those suffering as a result of poverty, sickness, bad housing, loneliness or discrimination.

Voluntary Work

Home Start, 2 Salisbury Road, Leicester LE1 7QR. Offers help to families with pre-school children who are experiencing difficulty coping.

Hospices, Most Hospices welcome volunteers to carry out a variety of work, including running activities in a day centre, patient care, administrative and office work, fundraising.

National Society for the Prevention of Cruelty to Children (NSPCC), 67 Saffron Hill, London EC1N 8RS. Gives practical help to families with children at risk.

Victims' Help Line, St Leonard's, Nuttall Street, London N1 5LZ. Gives support to people who are the victims of crime and who are left feeling very insecure and vulnerable.

Women's Royal Voluntary Service (WRVS), 234–244 Stockwell Road, London SW9 9SP. Works with those in need by providing a range of services, eg Meals on Wheels, Books on Wheels, Visiting Schemes, Driving Schemes, Crisis Support Schemes.

Group 3

These are a few of the many organisations that give support to people suffering from a particular illness, offering friendship and as much practical help as possible. They also raise money for medical research.

Arthritis and Rheumatism Council (ARC), 41 Eagle Street, London WC1R 4AR.

British Heart Foundation, 102 Gloucester Place, London W1H 4DH

Cancer Research Campaign, 2 Carlton House Terrace, London SW1Y 5AR

Leukaemia Research Fund, 43 Great Ormond Street, London WC1N 3JJ

Multiple Sclerosis Society of Great Britain and Northern Ireland, 25 Effie Road, London SW6 1EE

National Deaf Children's Society, 45 Hereford Road, London W2 5AH

Parkinson's Disease Society, 36 Portland Place, London W1N 3DG

Spastics Society, 12 Park Crescent, London W1N 4EQ

Group 4
These organisations work to improve the quality of life of the disabled by widening their social contacts and giving them the chance to experience different activities.

Camphill Village Trust Ltd Delraw House, Aldenham, Watford, Hertfordshire WD2 8DJ or Gawain House, 56 Welham Road, Norton, North Yorkshire YD17 7DP. Assists mentally handicapped adults towards independence and integration with the community at large.

Guide Dogs for the Blind Association, Alexandra House, 9 Park Street, Windsor, Berkshire SL4 1JR. Trains guide dogs for the blind and blind people in the use of such dogs. Association entirely dependent on voluntary financial support from the public and through the work of fund-raising branches.

PHAB (Physically Handicapped and Able Bodied), PHAB Centre, Bushland Road, Northampton NN3 2NS. Aims to further the integration of the physically disabled into the community. Promotes opportunities for the physically disabled and the able bodied to meet on equal terms.

Riding for the Disabled Association, Avenue 'R', National Agricultural Centre, Kenilworth, Warwickshire CV8 2LY. Gives disabled people the opportunity to gain confidence through riding.

Talking Newspaper for the Blind. For a list of local organisations, contact Talking Newspaper for the Blind Association of the United Kingdom, 90 High Street, Heathfield, East Sussex TN21 8JD.

Voluntary Work

Group 5

Many of the organisations which help people in need in Third World countries and the victims of disasters such as earthquakes and floods are very well known. Some of them also help people in need in Britain. They all rely on fund raising in this country.

Christian Aid, PO Box 100, London SE1 7RT

Ockenden Venture and Ockenden Venture Family Trust, Ockenden, Guildford Road, Woking, Surrey GU22 7UU

Oxfam, 274 Banbury Road, Oxford OX2 7DZ

Save the Children Fund, Mary Datchelor House, 17 Grove Lane, London SE5 8RD

War on Want, 37–39 Great Guildford Street, London SE1 0ES

World Vision of Britain, Dychurch House, 8 Abingdon Street, Northampton NN1 2AJ. Inter-denominational Christian relief and development agency to aid the hungry, homeless, poor and sick in over 60 developing countries.

Group 6

These associations are concerned with education or the arts.

Adult Literacy and Basic Skills Unit, 229–331 High Holborn, London WC1V 7DA. Helps adults with reading, writing, spelling and numeracy. Much of the teaching is carried out by volunteers on a one-to-one basis or in small groups.

Arts Association. Most areas have their own arts associations. They may belong to the National Association of Arts Centres, Room 110, The Arts Centre, Vane Terrace, Darlington, County Durham DL3 7AX.

Third Age Trust/University of the Third Age (U3A), 1 Stockwell Green, London SW9 9JF. Provides self-help educational activities among retired people of all ages.

Group 7

These organisations offer a range of services including first aid, nursing, training courses and services to people who are ill or in hospital.

The British Red Cross Society, 9 Grosvenor Crescent, London SW1X 7EJ. Provides first aid facilities at public events, gives instruction in first aid, provides a range of services to those in hospitals and day centres, eg beauty and manicure, hospital library etc.

Hospital League of Friends. Contact local hospital. Provides extra services for those in hospital, eg shop, refreshments, library service, flowers etc.

St John Ambulance, 1 Grosvenor Crescent, London SW1X 7EF. Provides first aid at public events, gives instruction in first aid, provides home nursing etc.

Group 8

A number of organisations are concerned with the welfare of animals and the environment. They include:

Council for the Protection of Rural England, Warwick House, 25 Buckingham Palace Road, London SW1W 0PP

Friends of the Earth, 26–28 Underwood Street, London N1 7JQ. Aims to conserve the planet's resources, reduce pollution and improve the quality of life

National Trust for Places of Historic Interest or National Beauty, 36 Queen Anne's Gate, London SW1H 9AS

Royal Society for the Prevention of Cruelty to Animals (RSPCA), The Causeway, Horsham, Sussex RH12 1HG

Royal Society for the Protection of Birds (RSPB), The Lodge, Sandy, Bedfordshire SG19 2DL

British Trust for Conservation Volunteers, 36 St Mary's Street, Wallingford, Oxfordshire OX10 0EU

Many organisations which do not fit comfortably into these groups include:

Voluntary Work

The Guide Movement, 17–19 Buckingham Palace Road, London SW1W 0PT

Scout Association, Baden-Powell House, Queen's Gate, London SW7 5JS

Royal National Lifeboat Institution (RNLI), West Quay Road, Poole, Dorset BH15 1HZ

Amnesty International, 99–119 Rosebery Avenue, London EC1R 4RE. A pressure group working for human rights.

Gingerbread, 35 Wellington Street, London SW2E 7BN. Provides day-to-day emotional support, practical help and social activities for lone parents and their children.

Voluntary Services Overseas, 317 Putney Bridge Road, London SW15 2PN. Aims to help Third World development by providing opportunities for people with skills to make a practical and individual contribution on a volunteer basis. No rigid upper age limit provided applicant is fit and suitable in other ways.

Be prepared

Some of the organisations listed in this chapter have to be particularly careful to appoint the right person for the job. This applies mainly to counselling organisations where the work can be very stressful, and it is as much for the good of the volunteer as for the client that great care is taken in selection. Counselling work requires people with understanding and compassion who can avoid becoming too involved with the client's problems – a difficult combination!

Other ways of participating in the community

We have looked at some of the voluntary organisations that work at national and local levels. Equally important to the community are activities which can be called public service, for example:

- *Councils*. If you are interested in how your local community is

run, you feel strongly about the decisions taken and want to make your views known, and you enjoy meetings, you could be a possible candidate for your local parish, district or County Council
- *Political Associations.* Anyone who feels strongly committed to a particular political party should contact the relevant political association who would be glad of their services.
- *Magistracy.* You no longer have to wait until someone proposes that you become a magistrate. If you are interested in the work, find out more from the Magistrates' Clerk's Office
- *Special Constabulary.* The upper age limit for entry is 50. Men should be not less than 5ft 6in and women 5ft 4in. Special constables make up the police reserve and are trained to undertake regular officers' routine policing duties when required. Uniform is provided free and expenses paid. Contact the nearest police headquarters.
- *Home Defence.* The upper age limit for entry to the Home Defence Force is 50 and you have to have had two years' previous experience in the regular Armed Forces, the Territorial Army or other part-time forces. The purpose of Home Defence is to be trained to defend key positions in this country in time of war. Payment is given for training and there is an annual bounty.

The scope for getting more involved in the community, whether paid or unpaid, is wide. Most organisations need more volunteers – the opportunities are there.

Case studies
   Brian's job as a long-distance lorry driver came to an end far earlier than he had anticipated, when, at the age of 56, he had a heart attack. The job had suited him well, though he was beginning to find it increasingly stressful.
   He did not feel ready to retire and was getting very depressed. Staying at home all the time after a job like his certainly did not suit him and he felt he still had a lot to offer. Then, one day, he was asked to drive a minibus of handicapped children to the sea for the day. He agreed rather half-heartedly. That day was the turning point for him. He was so impressed by the spirit of the severely handicapped

Voluntary Work

children that he determined to make the best of his own situation. He still enjoyed driving and was given the go-ahead medically, so he offered his services to Age Concern. Very soon he was driving three or four days a week for them and getting great satisfaction from it.

Soon afterwards, Brian and three other unemployed people became involved in setting up an organisation called Helpmate on his housing estate (which, with an unemployment rate of 17 per cent, had an increasing number of social problems). Helpmate encouraged unemployed people, whatever their ages, to come forward and offer to do a job for someone less able than themselves. Gradually, the idea developed. Some people offered to do painting and decorating, others gardening. One young lad with a bike offered to run a prescription collection service for the housebound or mothers with young children.

Helpmate became a registered charity with the support of the Youth Service and the Social Services. After much persuasion, the Council agreed to give them a flat rent free as their headquarters, and this enabled them to do much more. They set up a baby clinic once a week for the benefit of young mothers who found beforehand that the nearest clinic was too far away. The flat has become a drop-in centre at certain times of the week and people are encouraged to use it for different activities. One room has been set up as a dark room to be used by anyone on the estate.

For some, voluntary work has been a way back to paid employment as it has restored their self-confidence and motivation. One man in his fifties who had been made redundant from an engineering firm took a job as a caretaker at a school for handicapped children, something he would never have thought of before. Another man of 56 whose life had revolved round work and the pub thought he was definitely on the scrap heap when he lost his job and began to let drink get the better of him. Brian encouraged him to get involved with Helpmate and several months later he got another job in a meat-processing factory.

Others, like Brian himself, are not trying to get back into paid employment. The work he is doing in the community is varied and rewarding and through it he has made many friends. He says he is 'not a man who can sit still. I've always worked. I can't sit around and get depressed'.

Demanding and often frustrating, yet fun and very rewarding – this was **Helen**'s experience when she gave a home to a puppy from Guide Dogs for the Blind for the first year of its life. Jacob arrived aged eight weeks with a diet sheet and a list of 'dos and don'ts' for his basic training. The aim was that after a year he should be well-mannered in the house, trained to walk on the lead on the left-hand side of his walker without pulling, familiar with buses and trains; he would never jump up at feeding time or growl when a bone was taken away and never make a mess in the street!

Before Helen was entrusted with Jacob, she was interviewed so that the organisation could make sure she would have sufficient time to look after him properly and treat him kindly without spoiling him. It was not a job for someone very emotional about animals because, at the end of the year, Jacob would go on to be fully trained before being matched to his permanent owner.

The organisation pays for the dog's food and any vet's bills there might be during the year. A member of staff visits at regular intervals to make sure everything is going well and is always available for help and support. Helen found this invaluable when Jacob came near to getting the better of her. He would walk through town on his lead behaving beautifully and then suddenly play 'dead dog', lying spread-eagled on the pavement and looking up with his big, rolling eyes. There was nothing like it for drawing a crowd – advice, sympathy for Jacob, mutterings about illness were all freely given!

During that first year he changed from a beautiful 'Andrex' type puppy to a strong young dog with great character: he had learnt the basics and was ready to go on. That was the hardest part for Helen, but Jacob seemed unconcerned by it. Training him had been a great experience and Helen said it had made her very much more aware of all the things which were new and frightening for a young dog. One of the great moments was introducing him to the beach and sand-dunes. As for making new friends – walking Jacob led to meeting and talking to so many different people! A fully trained guide dog is extremely valuable, so introducing it to the world during the first year of its life is a responsible job and not to be taken lightly.

Further information and help

The National Council for Voluntary Organisations has its head office at 26 Bedford Square, London WC1B 3HU (telephone 071-

Voluntary Work

636 4066). It is a national umbrella organisation for many voluntary bodies and provides excellent information services.

You will be able to find out through your local Council for Voluntary Service or the Rural Community Council what opportunities there are in your area, and talk to someone about the type of work you would like to do and the time you can give. Every effort will be made to find a suitable opening and what you have to offer will always be greatly appreciated. Remember, too, that if you see a need for a service, you can always set up a group to help meet that need. That is how many play-groups are started.

Voluntary Agencies Directory (Bedford Square Press). Produced by the National Council for Voluntary Organisations and available in most public libraries.

Contact the nearest Council for Voluntary Service or the Rural Community Council for further information.

CHAPTER 9
Education and Training

A change in approach

Changing patterns of employment are having a major impact on education and training. Schools, colleges and universities are having to look critically at the courses they run and the teaching methods being used. Training organisations, developed largely as a result of government schemes, have moved away from the classroom approach which many of their clients found daunting. It is an exciting, though often uncomfortable, time for people involved in education; for us, the consumers, the opportunities are expanding all the time.

Whereas in the past it seemed that everyone who wanted to study had to fit into the system, we are now moving towards a situation where the system is having to fit in with the needs of the individual. There are now many more short courses for people who need to retrain or update their skills; special routes into universities or polytechnics for people without the standard entry requirements; study skills courses to help people overcome their fears of coping with the work involved and opportunities to study at home. As older people become an increasingly important part of the workforce, colleges and training organisations are bound to respond.

There is a much greater awareness, too, of the special situation of many women who want to return to work once they no longer feel tied by family commitments. Some women find that after years spent in the home, their confidence in coping with a job is minimal. Getting back into the job market will probably mean going back to college first of all and this can be an obstacle for some. An organisation called 'The Women Returners' network' works to encourage colleges and employers to offer education and training courses that meet the needs of women in this situation. Some broad-based courses aim, among other things, to restore confidence and can often prove to be an excellent first step. It is much easier to start with a group of people in a similar situation.

Why start learning more?

You may have a clear-cut reason for taking a particular course, such as:

- to learn a new skill in order to improve your job prospects, eg if you are looking for office or administrative work it is important that you can use a word processor
- to update or widen skills, eg a course in artexing can broaden the scope of a painter and decorator
- to gain a qualification necessary for a particular job, eg City and Guilds 730 Further Education Teachers' Certificate for teaching in a college of further education
- to gain entry into a higher level course, eg if you want to take a degree course at a polytechnic but do not have the standard entry qualifications, you can take a one- or two-year Access course at your local college of further education, or an Adult Foundation course
- to prepare yourself for self-employment. There are many courses designed to help people set up their own businesses

If none of these reasons apply to you, it is well worth considering taking a course for enjoyment. Learning about something you are interested in can be very satisfying and it is a pity that many older people who have bad memories of school fight shy of it. It could be that your previous job was office bound and you want to learn a practical skill such as wood turning or upholstery, or that you missed the chance of taking a degree when you were younger and want to do so now. The scope is vast. As a bonus, you will probably find that you meet new people with similar interests.

Choosing the right course

One of the problems that a wide choice of courses brings is making the right choice to achieve your goal. If the course is for general interest, find out as much as you can about it from any leaflets available and if possible from the person running it. Most people running courses are quite happy to tell you about them; after all, they much prefer satisfied customers to people who come once or twice and then drop out. You can find out about courses in your area by:

- sending for your local college prospectus
- going to the nearest Adult Education Centre. They usually produce a list of courses for the year
- enquiring at the library
- going to the nearest information centre
- looking in the local paper. Many courses start in September, so look out for advertisements in late August

If you are choosing a course leading to a particular qualification, whether it be a stepping stone to a higher level course, a way of updating skills or a change of direction career-wise, it is well worth discussing your plans with someone who knows what is available. New courses and new routes are opening up and professional guidance can help you to start in the right direction and at the right level. You may find that your previous experience counts towards the qualification you are aiming for and you will be exempt from some parts of the course.

It is very important, too, to test the reality of your plans. It is easy to generalise, but dangerous: each person needs individual professional guidance and information before taking what could be a very important step. You are making an important investment in time and money, so make sure, as far as possible, that the opportunities will be there at the end and that the course does not lead you up a blind alley.

Professional advice is available from several sources, including:

The careers service. Most careers services now offer guidance to adults as well as young people. Some services now advertise

Education and Training

'all age' guidance, while in other areas there is a special unit for adults.

Education guidance services. These services are expanding but are not yet available everywhere. They have been set up to help adults find out about the learning opportunities available and decide which option suits them best. A directory of services is published every year and a free copy can be obtained from:
ECCTIS
PO Box 88
Walton Hall
Milton Keynes MK7 6DB
A copy should be available in your library.

Local colleges. An increasing number of colleges are offering a guidance service. Contact your local college of further education.

Private guidance agencies. Advice is available but a fee is charged. Private agencies are listed in the Yellow Pages.

How computers can help

During the last few years there has been an increase in the number of computer databases storing a vast amount of information about courses. They include:

1. TAPS (Training Access Points). This is a database of training and educational opportunities. It includes information on open learning.
2. PICKUP (Professional, Industrial and Commercial Updating). The training information on this database is mainly intended to help people in work update their skills.
3. ECCTIS (Educational Counselling and Credit Transfer Information Service). This database has information on almost 80,000 courses in the UK.

Host Careers Services, Jobcentres, libraries and Training Centres have access to databases. It is important to combine this resource with personal guidance.

Return to learning

Starting a course which involves reading, taking notes, discussions and essay writing can be quite daunting for someone who has not had to do any formal study for a long time. Try not to be put off by this. Help is there! There is a much greater awareness of the need for study skills these days and many courses include an introduction to effective learning.

Many short courses concentrate solely on giving people the confidence to tackle studying again.

- Your local college may run short courses in study skills which would be a good preparation for whatever you were planning to do
- The *National Extension College* offers a series of very useful booklets on studying. Titles include:
  - 'Learning to Study.' Gives a realistic – and reassuring – taste of study to anyone wondering whether to embark on a course.
  - 'Clear Thinking'. A guide to preparing clear and logical essays and reports.
  - 'How to Write Essays'. Covers all the stages of successful essay writing, from making rough notes to writing up the final essay.
  - 'Reading and Understanding'. Helps students tackle the types of reading they are likely to encounter on a course of study.
  - 'Examination Skills'. Helps with exam preparation, gives advice on how to control exam nerves and suggests techniques to use during the exam.

    Further information and copies are available from:
    National Extension College
    18 Brooklands Avenue
    Cambridge CB2 2HN
    0223 316644

    Alternatively, copies may be available through an Open Learning centre at your local college
- *Open University*. Offers preparation courses to help people get back into studying before they start a degree course

Education and Training

Ways of study

Not only is there a vast range of courses available, but also an ever widening choice of how and where to study. Let us look at some of the organisations involved in education and training and see how they differ in what they have to offer.

1. Colleges of further education

These colleges used to be called technical colleges. They provide a wide range of courses at different levels up to, but not including, degree courses. Courses lead to many qualifications, from general education (GCSEs and A levels) to training for jobs. They also run courses for enjoyment or recreation. The emphasis in most colleges tends to be on technical, commercial and vocational subjects.

Courses may be full time, but there is an increasing number of part-time courses and evening classes.

In theory, most courses are open to anyone over 16, but those run specifically for older people are in the minority. The majority of students on general education courses are in the 16–19 age group. However, mature students are usually welcomed because they add a good balance to any group.

A course taken at a college of further education may be an end in itself or it may lead to a higher education course at a polytechnic or university. If you are aiming to take a degree course at a polytechnic or university but have not got the required entry qualifications, you may be able to join an Access course or an Adult Foundation course.

Access course
Access courses are usually set up by a college in conjunction with a university, polytechnic or college of higher education to provide a fast route for those who want to take a particular degree course but do not have the standard entry requirements. There are many subjects to choose from but they may not all be available in your area. Most of them are for one year and may be full or part time. They include counselling and help with study skills.

Adult Foundation course
These are similar to Access courses except that they prepare students for a number of further courses rather than a particular one.

Many colleges offer flexible learning as an alternative way to study. This can be Open Learning with tutorial support or a combination of classroom or seminar teaching and Open Learning.

For information about courses at your nearest college of further education, send for a college prospectus.

2. Open Learning

Open Learning or Distance Learning is a relatively new approach to study which has developed from correspondence courses. It consists of:

(a) Course material in the form of coursebooks, which are usually very well set out (quite different in approach from the school textbooks you might remember!), audio-cassettes and video tapes where appropriate.
(b) Tutorial support. This is usually available through the college or training organisation which provided you with the course. Sometimes it is by correspondence.
(c) Assignment or projects which are marked and assessed. Some courses lead to examinations.

Thousands of Open Learning courses are available, produced by many different organisations including Open College, the National Extension College, polytechnics, universities, training organisations etc. Some courses are much better produced than others and there is a wide price range. Selecting the right Open Learning course requires help and, if possible, you should go to an Open Learning centre for advice. Once you have selected a course, you take it away with you and work at your own pace and in your own home – ideally you should be linked to a tutor who will arrange times to meet and discuss your progress, either individually or in a group. Sometimes, this has to be done by correspondence or phone.

This way of studying has advantages and disadvantages. Let us look at some of them:

Advantages
- You can work at your own pace rather than that of a group
- You can choose when and where you work
- You can start a course whenever you choose
- You are not restricted to college terms
- It is a very good alternative for people who do not want to go back to college
- It can be very convenient for people who live in remote areas or who do not have transport

Disadvantages
- Not all Open Learning courses lead to a nationally recognised qualification. It is important to check this carefully
- Working on your own requires much more motivation than attending a regular course
- You do not have the stimulus of a group
- Open learning courses are expensive
- They are not so suitable for practical subjects

Some courses are a halfway house between Open and traditional learning. Computing courses, for example, often fall into this category. Many Open Learning centres, colleges and training organisations have computer centres where you can work at your own pace through a series of Open Learning courses, using their equipment and with a tutor usually close at hand. This can be a very satisfactory method of learning.

3. Adult education

Adult education under the management of the local education authority may be closely linked with a college of further education or run separately from an Adult Education Centre. The courses are mainly recreational and for interest, and run in response to local needs. They may be evening classes, part-time day classes, summer schools or residential courses.

The Workers' Educational Association (WEA) offers part-time

courses for adults. These do not usually lead to formal qualifications. For further information, contact the WEA branch secretary – the local library should be able to give you his or her name.

4. Training organisations

There are many training organisations offering a wide range of courses. Most of them developed to provide the training element of government schemes but have since broadened their scope and now offer courses to employed and unemployed people.

Many training organisations are run as private businesses and standards vary. It is important to establish as carefully as you can that you are going to get value for money.

5. Polytechnics

You may have noticed several changes taking place in third level education. Previously the fundamental difference between a university and a polytechnic was that a university had the power to award degrees at its own discretion. Polytechnics, on the other hand, had their degrees awarded by the Council for National Academic Awards (CNAA). The CNAA has now been abolished and all polytechnics have been given university status. At the time of going to press, most have changed their names to reflect this but a few have yet to agree satisfactory new titles. Many colleges provide a wide range of degree courses and Higher National Diploma (HND) courses, both academic and vocational. They also run postgraduate and professional courses and some provide one-year preparatory courses which enable students to reach a sufficiently high standard in certain subjects to start a degree course. Many are now also making provision for part-time study.

6. Universities

Universities offer a wide range of degree courses. To find out what courses are available, consult *The Compendium of University Entrance Requirements*, available at careers offices and libraries. Prospectuses for individual colleges give more detailed information.

Education and Training

7. Open University

The Open University offers first degree courses and diploma courses on an Open Learning basis. There are no minimum entry requirements.

The four elements are:

- course materials – books, audio tapes, TV programmes, videos
- regular meetings with tutors and counsellors at a study centre
- summer school for one week each year
- continuous assessment and an exam

The courses are built up on a modular basis, each module earning you a full or half credit. Six credits are needed for an ordinary degree and eight credits for an honours degree. This system enables you to choose the elements of your course as you go along.

It is possible to study the degree courses for interest, without taking the exams, as an associate student.

The academic year for the Open University is from February to November and you should apply at least six months before you want to start. It is difficult to get a local education authority grant, but the Open University has a special fund to help unemployed people.

For further information about courses, write for:

> Guide for Applicants for BA Degrees
> Admissions Office
> Open University
> PO Box 48
> Milton Keynes MK7 6AB

or for:

> Single courses and self-contained study packs
> Associate Student Central Office
> Open University
> PO Box 76
> Milton Keynes MK7 6AN

8. University of the Third Age

This aims to involve older people in teaching and organising research as well as learning by forming 'mutual aid' learning groups. It does not offer courses leading to qualifications.

For further information, contact:
> The Executive Secretary
> University of the Third Age
> 1 Stockwell Green
> London SW9 9JF

9. Adult Residential Colleges

Eight adult residential colleges offer high quality academic courses (mainly in humanities and social sciences) to adults wanting to study in order to go on to higher education (degree or HND) or to take a course as an end in itself. Most of the courses are one or two years in length, though there are shorter ones. No formal entry qualifications are required. Financial support is available in the form of an Adult Education State Bursary. The grant covers fees, residence and maintenance and allowances for dependants. For further information, write to the registrar of the individual college:

Coleg Harlech, Harlech, Gwynedd LL46 2PU
Co-operative College, Stanford Hall, Loughborough, Leicestershire LE12 5QR
Fircroft College, Bristol Road, Selly Oak, Birmingham B29 6LH
Hillcroft College, South Bank, Surbiton, Surrey KT6 6DF
Newbattle Abbey College, Dalkeith, Midlothian EH22 3LL
Northern College, Watworth Castle, Stainborough, Barnsley, South Yorkshire S75 3ET
Plater College, Pullers Lane, Oxford OX3 0DT
Ruskin College, Oxford OX1 2HE

Finance

It is one thing to want to study and another to pay for it! Financial assistance in the form of a grant or loan may be available in some circumstances.

- The Department for Education produces a booklet called

Education and Training

'Grants to Students – a brief guide' which is available from your local education authority or from:

The Department for Education
Room 4/50
Elizabeth House
York Road
London SE1 7PH

Mandatory grants must be paid to anyone taking a designated course provided certain conditions are satisfied, for example if you are taking a degree course for the first time (other than an Open University degree).

- *Discretionary grants* are awarded for some further education and part-time courses and you should apply to your local education authority. There is no general rule about the awarding of discretionary grants – it sometimes depends on which part of the country you live in.
- *Training and Enterprise Council (TEC) funding.* Some short courses are funded by the TEC in your area and there is no charge to the student. This applies to most Business Enterprise courses designed to help people set up their own business.
- *Loans.* Some banks are prepared to give loans on favourable terms for study, eg Career Development Loans. Enquire at your bank.
- Some colleges of further education *reduce or waive fees* for unemployed people. Enquire at your local college.
- *Educational charities* may be prepared to give a grant towards courses or equipment though these are usually small and aimed at young people. Refer to *The Directory of Grant-Making Trusts* (Charities Aid Foundation).
- *21-hour rule.* This applies in some areas. The scheme enables people who are unemployed to study for up to 21 hours a week without paying fees provided they remain available for work. However, it is not as simple as it sounds and is likely to change! Consult your local college or Jobcentre.

Case studies

Jennifer had not been in paid employment since she had her first child at the age of 27. Twenty years later she was keen to develop a career for herself. Her children had left home and she and her husband had recently separated.

She had always been interested in social work and felt that she had a lot to contribute when it came to understanding people's problems and giving advice and information. For several years she had been working at the Citizens' Advice Bureau two days a week. She went along to discuss the possibilities with a careers adviser and discovered that to become a professional Field Social Worker she would have to take a two-year course leading to a Diploma in Social Work. She was told that courses specifically intended for mature students did not demand the standard entry requirements but that she would have a much better chance of being offered a place if she had evidence of recent study to show that she would be able to cope with the course.

This was how Jennifer came to enrol for A level Sociology at her local college of further education. She found reading, making notes and writing essays very hard work for the first term but a study skills course helped and she is now very much more confident. She is finding the course very interesting and enjoys being in a class with young people. In fact there is one other mature student, so she is not alone. She hopes she will be accepted at a polytechnic to take the Diploma in Social Work course and sees that as an exciting challenge.

Michael wanted to become an expert in something outside work. He had never had the opportunity or the time to learn about anything in depth and felt the need to find something he could really get involved in. He did not want to measure his expertise against others; it was purely for his own satisfaction.

Once he had chosen to study Italian Culture he started to plan his own programme. This made him much more aware of what was going on locally. For example, whereas he had been used to popping into the library to borrow a book from time to time, he now took a new look at ways of using the library. He started to consult the staff whom he found very willing to help and whom he now feels he has got to know well. He used the reference library as well as the lending library and found it a good place to settle down to read for an afternoon. The atmosphere helped his concentration. He found out about courses run at his local college and enrolled for the one he felt would be most useful to start with. This has given him the chance to meet others with the same interest. He may consider taking an Open University course later on as an associate member. In the meantime, he has made a definite commitment and is very enthusiastic about what he has undertaken.

Further information and help

Second Chances (COIC)

Mature Students. Entry to Higher Education, Bell, Hamilton and Roderick (Longman)

Never Too Late to Learn, Bell and Roderick (Longman)

Back to Work: A Guide for Women Gemma O'Connor (Macdonald Optima)

Returning to Work, A Practical Guide for Women, Alec Reed (Kogan Page)

The Kogan Page Mature Student's Handbook, Margaret Korving (Kogan Page)

'University Degree Courses for Mature Students'. Free leaflet from UCCA, PO Box 28, Cheltenham, Gloucestershire GL50 1HY

Directory of Further Education (CRAC Hobson's)

Polytechnic Courses Handbook (The Committee of Directors of Polytechnics)

Compendium of University Entrance Requirements (Association of Commonwealth Universities)

Part-Time Degrees, Diplomas and Certificates (CRAC Hobson's)

Open Learning Directory (The Training Agency)

'Paying for Training' (DES). A comprehensive guide to sources of finance for adult training.

UK Directory of Educational Guidance Services for Adults (Unit for the Development of Adult Continuing Education (UDACE))

CHAPTER 10
Government Initiatives

There have been considerable changes in the provision made to help unemployed people get back into work during the last couple of years. The many different schemes and opportunities funded by the Department of Employment are clearly explained in leaflets available in Jobcentres. One of the results of the Citizen's Charter is that Jobcentres are committed to providing clear information about their services which range from giving help in applying for jobs to training in new job skills.

Anyone who is unemployed and looking for work should call at their local Jobcentre and ask to see a New Client Adviser. New client advisers are specially trained to advise people on their next move and they help you to draw up a Back to Work plan, setting out how you can best help yourself and make use of the opportunities provided. Advisers will also make sure you are claiming the benefits you are entitled to.

If you have not succeeded in finding work within three months you will have the opportunity to review your Back to Work plan. You may ask to have an interview with a Claimant Adviser who is an expert on the local job market and on the benefits you can claim in work. There are also options open to you after three months which you might decide to take up such as Job Search Seminars and Job Review Workshops. Taking part in these schemes will not affect the amount of money you receive and your travelling costs will be paid.

Job search seminars

Job search seminars, usually lasting for two days, provide expert help in looking for jobs and making applications. They also include guidance on improving your performance at interviews. You may take up the offer of further support on a 'drop in' basis for up to four weeks after attending a seminar.

Job review workshops

Job review workshops last for two days and give you the opportunity to look at alternative careers. They are designed for people who are looking for a career change and have a professional, executive or administrative background.

Travel to Interview Scheme

This scheme aims to help people who have been unemployed for four weeks or more to attend interviews by paying travelling expenses when the interview is beyond normal daily travelling distance. Application forms are available at Jobcentres.

There are further opportunities for people who have been unemployed for six months or more. Again benefit will not be affected and travelling costs will be paid.

Jobclubs

Anyone who has been unemployed for six months or more, whether in receipt of benefit or not, can join a Jobclub provided that they agree to attend regularly (usually four half days a week). There is a limit of 16 weeks but in certain circumstances this can be extended to 26 weeks. Each Jobclub has a leader who helps you look for jobs, prepare CVs and make job applications. The aim is to get everyone a job as quickly as possible and the theory is that the more applications you make the better your chances. You have free use of the telephone and are provided with free paper, pens and stamps. In addition, a photocopier and typewriter are available free of charge. Being in a small club (usually 15-20 people) helps members give each other support and encouragement.

Job Interview Guarantee (JIG)

Through this scheme you will be given help to improve your chances of getting a job through a short course on brushing up your applications and interview technique, specific training or work trials. Work trials give you a chance to try out a job and show an employer what you can do for up to three weeks. This will not affect your benefit. You will be guaranteed an interview with an employer at the end of this scheme.

Courses for considering the future

These were called Restart courses but now each area has its own name and course structure though the aims are the same. If you have been unemployed for a long time, a course like this, usually lasting for five days or ten half days, might help to restore your confidence and encourage you to look again at the range of jobs or training courses you might apply for.

Training and Enterprise Councils

In addition to the courses which are funded by the Department of Employment and are available country wide, training on a regional basis is provided by Training and Enterprise Councils (TECs). TECs aim to make sure that training opportunities exist so that people can develop and update their skills.

Throughout England and Wales there are 82 Training and Enterprise Councils which receive government funding and are free to draw up their own training programmes. As a result, there is much greater regional variation in provision than there was a few years ago under the Training Agency. In Scotland Local Enterprise Companies have a similar role. They are directed by top business and community leaders who have an overall knowledge of the employment needs of their area. As well as providing training to meet specific skill shortages, TECs fund courses of a more general nature, some of which might include work placements. All the courses should give trainees the opportunity to spend time on job search.

Women who want to return to work after a break in their careers will find there are courses funded by their local TECs specially tailored to their needs.

Courses for women returners

Although these courses may all have different names the content will be similar. Topics covered will include:

- the current employment scene and how to tackle it
- assessment and development of personal strengths
- general opportunities and support services
- individual guidance leading to an action plan
- work sampling
- writing a CV
- preparing for interviews
- looking at difficulties women may have when returning to work.

These courses help to boost confidence by enabling women to work in a group, share experiences and talk about their aims and their problems with others in a similar situation. They are run at colleges of further education or Training Centres.

Business and Enterprise Services

Another field that TECs specialise in is providing advice and training for unemployed people who want to set up and run their own businesses. Courses are available to help test the viability of a proposition, draw up a realistic business plan and provide information about grants and loans. You may be eligible for a grant called an Enterprise Allowance which is payable until your business starts to bring in a regular income. The amount is decided locally.

How to Get a Job After 45

Guidance

Some TECs are very aware of the importance of guidance and run advisory services for adults. If there is one in your area take advantage of it. A consultation with an adviser who can look at your situation realistically in the context of the local job market and lead you in the right direction is always worth while.

Ways of using the schemes

Make use of all that is available if it is going to be of help to you and remember that schemes and courses must be used to your advantage. Never let your needs come second to the needs of a training organisation. For example, don't be persuaded to enrol for a course that is not suitable simply because a training organisation has certain places it needs to fill.

It can be useful to use more than one scheme, eg:

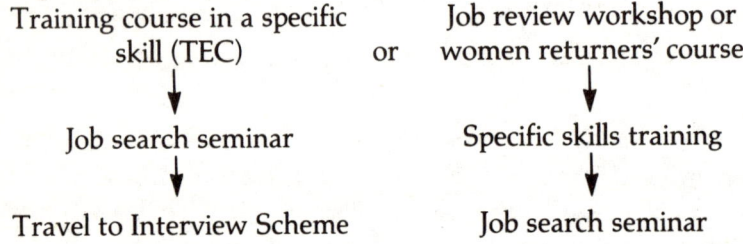

Above all, find out from your local Jobcentre and TEC what is available and make the most of it.

Case studies

Tim left the army last year, having completed his service, and was looking forward to starting a second career. He hoped to use his experience as an instructor in the army in civilian life and felt that this combined with his energy and determination would see him through. He had been instructing mainly in the use and making of videos, a field he finds extremely interesting.

He quickly found a job where he could use his experience but it turned out to be a very unsatisfactory situation and he left after three months.

Disillusioned by this experience, Tim decided to start his own business. He planned to set up a commercial enterprise to teach organisations how to make videos and make the best use of equipment that was often lying idle. He drew up a plan and applied for an Enterprise Allowance. He was turned down. The impression he received was that his plan was good and likely to be successful and therefore did not warrant a supporting grant; the powers that be, he felt, were more likely to give a grant to a business project that was likely to struggle. This was his first brush with bureaucracy!

Very soon after this Tim joined a six-month scheme called Employment Action, sponsored by the TEC. This scheme offers people temporary work to help maintain their skills. All work carried out has to benefit the local community in one way or another and participants are encouraged to set up their own project.

Tim's plan was to teach the disabled members of two day centres to make their own videos, combining lessons and lectures with practical hands-on experience. The response from the disabled was tremendous and he soon had an enthusiastic team working on a promotional video to be presented to the Social Services Department.

Tim hopes that the value of what he is doing will be recognised and that at the end of the scheme funding will be available so that day centres can buy in his services. He is confident that other council departments will buy in his services too – the Trading Standards Department are the first to make positive enquiries. How much better to have a video of an example of bad practice than to depend on verbal reports and witnesses. As a second string, he would like to become more involved in videoing sport.

Without Employment Action Tim would not have been able to get this far. He is able to make all his phone calls free from the Training Centre and can use the computer and photocopier for all his paperwork. In addition he has the strong moral support and backing of the training organisation.

He feels that six months, however, may not prove long enough and he finds the uncertainty worrying. What comes over very strongly in conversation with Tim is his determination to succeed and the way he is using the scheme to meet his needs.

Mary enrolled for the return to work course at the local College of Further Education with mixed feelings. Would she cope? Would she be much older than everyone else? Would she make a fool of herself? After all it was almost 15 years since she had worked in an office. She felt annoyed with herself for being torn between a need to get out and work and a lack of confidence that seemed to undermine her.

When she arrived on the first day she was relieved to see that the group did not consist entirely of 'young mums' but that there were several women about the same age as herself, or older. By the end of the first day she had chatted to quite a few people over coffee and lunch and discovered that most of them needed to restore confidence in their own ability.

She was pleasantly surprised that the tutor did not regard all that she had done at home over the years to have no value in a job situation. When she came to consider the skills she had developed she realised how important some of them would be in a working environment. That made her feel better straight away.

Offices had changed so much since she last worked that she never thought she would be able to go back to secretarial work. Computers were quite beyond her, she thought. Gradually she became aware that the assumptions she had made were wrong.

She discovered that there were courses, free of charge, where she could learn how to use a computer and update her office skills generally. The tutor arranged for her to join one of these courses for a day to see what it involved. She found this very helpful.

By the end of the return to work course Mary had decided to apply for an office skills course and get back to the work she had been so good at before. She felt confident that she would cope and was far more optimistic about her future.

CHAPTER 11
A Varied Life

Full-time work does not have to be the answer for everyone. If you can afford to look at other ways of using your time and the experience you have built up over the years there is plenty of opportunity ahead.

People find it easier to be busy than to have too much time on their hands, particularly if they have been used to the fairly rigid framework that a full-time job imposes. Jobs can, in a sense, be a protection from the demands of family and friends for whom working hours have been a 'no-go' area. Everything else had to be fitted around the job and now something else needs to be put in its place. Building up an alternative framework takes careful planning and will power.

Colin had to take early retirement and said he had to 'resist the temptation to be indolent' and to put off making decisions until another day. He found it more difficult than he had expected to cope without the stimulus and companionship of colleagues and without the week's structure he had become so used to. It was not easy, either, to learn to live on a restricted income and he had to look at ways of making the best possible use of what he had. He talked about the stage when he decided to take a positive approach and establish a way of life that would, in a sense, be a new career for him, although unpaid. He felt he still had the ability to achieve new goals and that the opportunities were there. Colin needed to take a fairly analytical approach to the problem. He realises this is not the way for everyone but emphasises the importance of taking the initiative instead of letting time slip by.

There are many women not in full-time employment who are accustomed to relying on their own resources to develop a full and varied life. They may combine paid part-time work with voluntary work, take a course for interest or to learn a skill, or spend time on a particular hobby. They illustrate how it is possible to control the way a person's pattern of life develops.

Marie, now 54, left her last full-time job ten years ago. With children still at school and planning to go to university she needed to contribute to the family income but she also needed more flexibility. She had agreed to make a home for her mother-in-law with the family, and as the elderly lady's health failed Marie had to devote more time to her.

Her first part-time job was as the local organiser of English courses for French students. She was responsible for arranging accommodation for the students with host families, planning visits and leisure activities, being on hand when the students were there to sort out problems that arose.

Marie did not need any particular qualifications for the job, but being a very diplomatic and caring person she was highly suitable. Though not essential, her office skills came in useful as there was a lot of paperwork involved. Perhaps one of the greatest challenges was working to a budget.

The busiest periods were when the students' booking forms arrived and there was a great deal to do in a short space of time, and during the courses when Marie felt she had to be 'on call' all the time. Otherwise, she was able to decide for herself how long she needed to spend each week. There were several months in mid winter when there was nothing to do.

This was one of several occupations. After her mother-in-law died, Marie became a landlady and took in a lodger. She enjoys the contact this brings. She became involved in voluntary work, which takes about one day a week, and she decided to take a wordprocessing course with a view to 'temping' in the future. It takes good organisation to weave the strands together but it does make for an interesting life.

There are men in their fifties and sixties in a position to build up a varied life in the same way, but many still feel that 'everybody else' expects them to get back into the traditional pattern of full-

A Varied Life

time work as soon as they can. This may not always be possible, let alone desirable. It is not 'giving-up' to look at different ways of making the best use of time. Sometimes it is just a question of being realistic.

If you are hoping to include part-time work in your new way of life you may find a job that is interesting and fulfilling. You may, on the other hand, have to settle for something tedious and routine because you need the money. If this is the case, try to balance your job with some form of unpaid activity where you feel you are doing something worth while and in which you are using your experience and skills. One will bring in some money; the other will bring a greater feeling of self-respect and achievement. Look at what else is going on in your area: you may well find some new interest now that you have the time. Getting involved in three or four different activities can be much more interesting than spending all your time in one job. Maybe this is the time to do it. It will certainly keep your mind active and put you in touch with a wide network of people. Colin said that he had become acquainted with over a hundred people he had not met before through becoming involved with different organisations.

This way of life does require more self-discipline than the traditional nine-to-five job where you had little choice about the role you had to perform. It is you who have to organise and motivate yourself. In return, you will have greater flexibility, more choice and more interest. Success should be measured in terms of the satisfaction you gain from life, not in terms of how others see you. Some things really are there for the taking.

Index

ACAS 103
Access courses 127
Accountancy, voluntary 109
Administrative work, voluntary 109
Advice and information, giving voluntary 109
Adult/Community Education Centre 23
Adult education 129
Adult Foundation Course 128
Adult Guidance Services 16
Adult Literacy and Basic Skills Unit 115
Adult Residential Colleges 132
Advertisements for jobs
Analysing 40-42
Advisory, Conciliation and Arbitration Service (ACAS) 103
Age and employment 19
Age Concern 112
Al-Anon Family Groups UK and Eire 111
Alcohol Recovery Project 112
Ambulance Service 109
Amnesty International 117
Analysing advertisements 40-42
Ancillary helper 77
Animals, voluntary work with 100
Application forms 52
Applications 'on spec' 53
Arthritis and Rheumatism Council 113
Arts Association 115
Automobile Association 65

Banks 91
Beauty care, voluntary 109
Blood sample collector 70
British Coal Enterprise Ltd 91
British Franchise Association 85, 91
British Heart Foundation 113
British Red Cross Society 109, 110, 116
British Steel Corporation 91
British Trust for Conservation, volunteers 116
Budget planner 25-6
Business in the Community 89

Camphill Village Trust Ltd 114
Cancer Research Campaign 113
Care assistant 71
Careers officer 74
Careers service 16, 21, 124
Caring jobs 70-74
Central Office of Information 26
Changing values 30-32
Christian Aid 115
Citizens' Advice Bureau 27, 110, 112
Civil Service 65
Club steward 69
Colleges of further education 23, 127
Community Alarm assistant 66
Community work 117-18
Consultant/interviewer with private employment agency 74
Cooperatives 86
Councils 117

147

Index

Council for the Protection of Rural England 116
Counselling, voluntary 109
Court usher 78
Cruse 109, 112
CVs 36, 38, 42, 44, 45, 46–52, 53

Department for Education 76, 132–3
Department of Social Security 105
Department of Transport 75
DIY, voluntary 110
Driving examiner 75
Driving instructor 75
Driving, voluntary 109

Education and training 122–35
    Choosing a course 124
    Finance 132–3
    Further information 135
    Returning to learning 126
    Ways of study 127
Education guidance services 125
Employment agencies 22
Employment Gazette 21
Enterprise Allowance 90, 139

Financial situation 23–7
First aid, voluntary 110
Fitness for work 33–4
Florist 68
Franchising 85–6
Freefone Enterprise 89
Freeline Social Security 27
Friends of the Earth 116
Fund raising, voluntary 110

Gingerbread 117
Glass-house grower 68
Government initiatives 136–42
    Enterprise Allowance 139
    Job interview guarantee 138
    Job review workshops 137
    Job search seminars 137
    Jobclubs 137
    Restart course 138
    Travel to Interview Scheme 137
Grants or loans 132–3
Guide Dogs for the Blind Association 114

Guide Movement The 117

Help the Aged 112
Home Defence 118
Home help 71
Home Office 79
Home Start 113
Home visiting, voluntary 109
Homecare assistant/nurse 71
Hospital driver 69
Hospital League of Friends 110, 116
Hospital porter 69
Housekeeper 69
Housing Benefit 24, 105
Housing Department 27, 74
Housing Officer 66

Imperial Cancer Research Fund 110
Income Support 24, 105, 111
Institute of Sales and Marketing Management 78
Interviews 57–60

Job interview guarantee 138
Job opportunities 63–82
    Caring 70–73
    Office/administration 64–8
    Practical 68–70
    Sales 77
    Security and protective services 78–82
    Teaching/training/guidance 74–7
Job review workshops 137
Job search seminars 137
Job sharing 100–101
Jobcentre 21, 24
Jobclubs 16, 137

Lecturer in college of further education or Adult Education Centre 76
Letters 42–6, 53–6
Leukaemia Research Fund 113
Life management 30–31
Local Enterprise Agencies 89
Local government 66–7
Looking back 28–30

Magistracy 118

Index

Market research 77
Medical receptionist 67
Medical records clerk 67
Minister of religion 71
Multiple Sclerosis Society of Great Britain and Northern Ireland 113

National Council for Voluntary Organisations 121
National Deaf Children's Society 114
National Extension College 126
National Insurance 105
National Society for the Prevention of Cruelty to Children 113
National Trust 116
National Trust administrator 67
Newspaper advertisements 22
Nursing auxiliary 71

Occupational therapy helper 72
Ockenden Venture and Ockenden Venture Family Trust 115
Office/administrative jobs 64–8
Open College 92
Open learning 23, 128–9
Open learning tutor 76
Open University 126, 131
Oxfam 110, 115

Parkinson's Disease Society 114
Partnership 86
Part-Time Careers Ltd 106
Part-time work 97–106
  Benefits 104–5
  Disadvantages 98–9
  Employment rights 102–3
  Job sharing 100–101
  National Insurance 105–6
  Permanent 99–100
  Seasonal work 101
  Temporary work 101
  Term-time working 102
PHAB 114
Phlebotomist 70
Physiotherapy helper 72
Placement officer 75
Polytechnics 130
Postwomen, postmen 69
Practical jobs 68–70

Prison Officer 78
Probation ancillary 72
Probation officer 72
Public speaking 110

Relate 110, 112
Retirement pension 105, 111
Riding for the Disabled Association 110, 114
Royal Automobile Club 65
Royal National Lifeboat Institution 117
Royal Society for the Prevention of Cruelty to Animals 116
Royal Society for the Protection of Birds 116
Rural Development Commission 90

St John Ambulance 109, 116
Sales assistant 77
Sales jobs 77–8
  Voluntary 110
Sales representative 78
Samaritans 109, 112
Save the Children Fund 115
School caretaker 69
Scottish Development Agency 90
Scout Association 117
Seasonal work 101
Second Chance 109
Secretarial work, voluntary 109
Secretary 68
Security officer 79
Self-employment 83–95
  Advice 89–91
  Business plan 88–9
  Enterprise Allowance 90, 139
  Franchising 85–6
  Ideas for 84–6
  Testing the market 87–8
  Training 91
Self-promotion 39–60
Skills assessment 35–7
Skills, updating 22–3
Small Firms Service 90
Social work assistant 73
Social worker 73
Spastics Society 114
Special Constabulary 118

Index

Speculative letters 53–55
Steward of sports club 69

Talking Newspaper for the Blind 114
Taxi driver 70
Teacher 76
Teaching, training and guiding 74–7
Teaching, voluntary 109
Temporary work 101
Term-time working 102
Third Age Trust/University of the Third Age 115
Tourist Boards 90
Traffic warden 79
Training Access Points 125
Training and Enterprise Councils 90, 91, 138, 139, 140
Training organisations 129
Training Officer 75
Travel to Interview Scheme 137
Tutor for Open Learning 77

Undertaker's assistant 70
Unemployment Benefit 24, 104, 110
University courses 130
University of the Third Age 131

Victims' Help Line 113
Voluntary Service Overseas 117
Voluntary work 107–21

War on Want 115
Warden of sheltered accommodation 74
Welsh Development Agency 90
Women Returners' Network 123
Women's Royal Voluntary Service 113
Workers' Educational Association 129
World Vision of Britain 115